Elementary A2

Louis Rogers

with additional material
by James Greenan

@work

Student's Book

Richmond

Contents

More practice = more practice available on the digital and print Workbook

Writing emails p44

	Language			Skills			
	Grammar / Functions	Vocabulary	Say it right	Listening	Reading	Speaking	Writing
6 Getting around p56							
It's quicker to walk	Present continuous	Travel		Four people talk about how they travel to work. Three people talk about why they are late	Four people talk about what they're doing this week	Talking about what you do every week and what you're doing this week	
Travel arrangements	Present continuous for future arrangements	Air travel	*s* at the end of a word	Larry talks about his business trip	An email about a business trip	Talking about your plans for the weekend	
On the move	Travelling by plane and train	Air and train travel		Three conversations at the airport. Three conversations at the train station		At the airport. At the train station	
Scenario: When and where? Marek, Magda and Rosie need to meet to discuss a new café.							
7 Shopping p64							
A career in retail	Past simple – *be* and regular verbs	Career and education	Past simple – regular verbs		A company description	Talking about the past	
Getting a bargain	Past simple – irregular verbs	Shopping			Three texts about shopping	Talking about what you did at the weekend	
Buying gifts	Shopping			Three people shopping in a department store	Gifts around the world	Shopping in a department store	
Scenario: A good location Christina and Paul want to start a business selling only British food.							
8 Getting it right p72							
Getting it wrong	Past simple – negative forms	Success and failure		Dal LaMagna's business successes and failures	Dal LaMagna – an American entrepreneur	Talking about mistakes	
The secret of my success		Characteristics for business success		Temi talks about success in business		Talking about successes	
Successful meetings	Meetings. Suggesting, giving opinions, agreeing and disagreeing	Talking about meetings		A meeting	Successful meetings	Suggesting, giving opinions, agreeing and disagreeing	
Scenario: A dysfunctional team Alex and Zafira put together a new team to develop and launch a new product.							
9 Best practice p80							
Company rules and dress code	*can* and *can't*, *have to* and *don't have to*	Company rules		Company rules		Talking about rules in your company	
Working conditions	Question forms with *can* and *have to*		*can* and *can't*	A supermarket manager talks about his working conditions	Two people talk about their working conditions	Talking about your job	
Email etiquette	Formal and informal emails	Starting and finishing an email			A formal and an informal email. Dos and don'ts of email etiquette		A formal and an informal email
Scenario: Problems at reception Youssef needs to sort out the problems at reception.							
10 A helping hand p88							
Making decisions	*will* for spontaneous decisions and promises			Lia talks to her mentor, José	Mentors	Making decisions	
Team building		Team roles			Creating a team	Discussing a team's strengths and weaknesses	
Suggestions and offers	Suggestions and offers			Three conversations where people make suggestions and offers. A phone call discussing suggestions	Emails making suggestions		A formal email
Scenario: In need of help Abdulrahman needs to arrange a team building exercise.							

Introductions

Pleased to meet you

present simple *be*
possessive adjectives
personal information

OSAKA

MONTEVIDEO

SYDNEY

Start up

1 Look at the cities on the map. Which countries are they in? Which of the cities do you know?

Reading

2 🔊 1.1 Read and listen. Check your answers to **1**.

SYDNEY

This is Karen Wood. She's 43 years old. She's an engineer for Alsthom in Sydney, Australia. She's married. Her husband's a software designer. His name's Sanjit. He's from Pune in India.

OSAKA

This is Yuji Kamasaki. He's 29 years old and he's a sales representative for Nissan. He's single. He works at the Nissan offices in Osaka in the south of Japan, but Yuji's originally from the north of the country. His hometown's Morioka.

MONTEVIDEO

This is Santiago Ramos and this is Rosa Perez. They're from Montevideo and they're both computer programmers for Microsoft Uruguay. They're married and their partners also work for Microsoft. Rosa's husband is an administrator and Santiago's wife is a director.

Listening

3 🔊 1.2 Santiago Ramos is in Los Angeles for a conference. Listen and complete his registration form.

REGISTRATION FORM	
First name	
Surname	
Date of birth	
Occupation	
Nationality	
Address	*Calle Andes Nol 892 Piso 3, 111000 Montevideo*

4 Listen again and complete the questions.

1 Can I .... you some questions?
2 What's .... surname?
3 .... are you from?
4 .... your date of birth?
5 .... your job?
6 Can I .... your home address, please?

Speaking

5 Interview another student and complete the registration form. Begin like this:

Can I ask you some questions?
Yes, of course.

REGISTRATION FORM	
First name	
Surname	
Date of birth	
Occupation	
Nationality	
Address	

Grammar

Present simple *be*	
Long form	Short form
I am	I'm
You are	You're
He/She/It is	He's/She's/It's
We are	We're
They are	They're

More practice

>>>GRAMMAR REFERENCE PAGE 102

6 Complete the sentences with the correct form of *be*.

1 I'......... from Brazil.
2 They'......... from Australia.
3 I'......... a manager.
4 We'......... American.
5 She'......... a software engineer.
6 It'......... in Australia.

7 ◀))) 1.3 Listen and check your answers. Practise the pronunciation.

Listening

8 ◀))) 1.4 Santiago meets a friend at the conference. Listen and answer the questions.

1 What's his friend's name?
2 Where's he from?
3 What's his job?

?

possessive *'s*
Santiago's friend
His friend's name is Paul.

9 Complete the text. Check your answers in audioscript 1.4 on page 114.

This ....¹ my colleague Rosa.
We work together in ....² .
Rosa, this ....³ my old
......................⁴ Chintal Patel from Sydney.
We were at university together. He's a
......................⁵ with Dell.

Hello, Chintal, nice to ....⁶ you.

Hello, Rosa, good to ....⁷ you, ...⁸ .

Speaking

10 Introduce yourself to the person on your right. Ask him/her about where he/she is from and what his/her job is. Introduce him/her to the person on your left.

?

Introducing yourself
I'm [name].
This is [name].
Nice to meet you.
Good to meet you, too.

Grammar

Possessive adjectives			
I	→ my	she	→ her
you	→ your	we	→ our
he	→ his	they	→ their

More practice

>>>GRAMMAR REFERENCE PAGE 102

11 Complete the sentences with the correct possessive adjective.

1 'What's .... job?' 'He's a restaurant manager.'
2 I'm single and I live at home with .... parents.
3 Can you give me .... home address, please?
4 'Those are my children in the photo.' 'Really? What are .... names?'

Writing

12 Write a profile of a friend or colleague (40–50 words). Use the first text in **9** to help you. Begin like this:

This is ... He/she ...

Start up

1 Complete the sentences with different nationalities.

1 My mobile phone is ....
2 My car is ....
3 My television is ....
4 My company is ....
5 My favourite food is ....

2 Complete the sentences with the nationalities in the box.

Argentinian	Brazilian	Chinese	French	German	Indian	Japanese	Spanish

1 Mercedes is a .... car manufacturing company.
2 Sony is a .... electronics company.
3 Curry is an .... food.
4 Rio de Janeiro is an .... city.
5 Louis Vuitton is a .... clothes designer.
6 Messi is a .... soccer star.
7 Madrid is a .... city.
8 Shanghai is a .... city.

?

articles
Tata is **an** Indian car company.
an is used with vowels a, e, i, o and u
BMW is **a** German car manufacturer.
a is used with consonants, e.g. b, c, d, f

Say it right **3** Write the countries and nationalities in the correct column.
Compare your answers with a partner.

America American	Brazil Brazilian	Britain British	China Chinese	Germany German
India Indian	Japan Japanese	Mexico Mexican	Portugal Portuguese	Spain Spanish

○	○o	o○	○oo	oo○	o○oo
1 Spain	**2** Britain	**3** Brazil	**4** Germany	**5** Japanese	**6** America
....	....	....	....	....	....
....	....	....	....		....
....		....	....		
....			....		
			....		

4 ◗))) 1.5 Listen and check

Speaking **5** Work with a partner. Make true sentences about the people, places and companies using nationalities and the words in the box.

city	company	politician	tennis player	writer

1 Sony
  Sony is a Japanese company.
2 Rafael Nadal
3 Cairo
4 Barack Obama
5 Shakespeare

Listening

6 🔊 **1.6** Listen and match conversations 1–3 with photos a–c.

7 Listen again. Complete the phrases from the conversations.

1 Receptionist: Is that a Spanish name?
Customer: No, ... Spanish. It's Portuguese.
2 Passport officer: Are you here on holiday?
Traveller: No, ... We're here for a conference.
3 Receptionist: Which department .... in, please?
Customer: He's in the sales department.
Receptionist: One moment, please … I'm sorry, ...
at his desk at the moment. Can I take a message?

a
b
c

Grammar

Present simple *be*	Negative and question forms
Negative long form	**Short form**
I am not	I'm not
You are not	You aren't
He/She/It is not	He/She/It isn't
We are not	We aren't
They are not	They aren't

Questions		
Are you French?	Yes, I am. / No, I'm not.	Where are you from?
Is it time for lunch?	Yes, it is. / No, it isn't.	When's lunch?
Are they happy?	Yes, they are. / No, they aren't.	What's the problem?

》》GRAMMAR REFERENCE PAGE 102

8 Complete the questions. Use the information in brackets to write an answer.
1 it / a Spanish company? (✗) *Is it a Spanish company? No, it isn't.*
2 you / a computer expert? (✗) ....
3 he / married? (✓) ....
4 they / here for the conference? (✓) ....
5 she / the company director? (✗) ....
6 Who / the / CEO? (Ana Leon) ....
7 Where / you / from? (Brazil) ....
8 Which / car / yours? (Audi) ....

More practice

Say it right

9 🔊 **1.7** Listen and repeat the alphabet.

a b c d e f g h i j k l m n o p q r s t u v w x y z

10 Write the letters of the alphabet in the correct place according to the sound.

/eɪ/	A H	/əʊ/	O
/iː/	B C	/uː/	Q ..... W
/e/	F I	/ɑː/	R
/aɪ/	I		

11 🔊 **1.8** Listen and check.

12 🔊 **1.9** Listen and write the names of the six people and places you hear.

Speaking

13 Work with a partner. Write down the names of three people and three places. Take turns to spell the words for your partner to write.

14 Work in pairs. Student A, look at page 96. Student B, look at page 98.

Start up ① Work with a partner. Look at the expressions. Which ones do you use:

1 when you arrive somewhere?
2 when you leave?

Hi

Good morning

Good night

See you soon

Bye

Goodbye

Have a safe journey

How are you?

Hello

Listening ② **1.10** Listen and match conversations 1–4 with pictures a–d.

③ Listen again and complete the conversations.

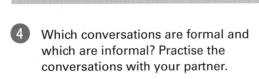

1 A: Hello. Good .... , everybody.
   B: Hello, Mrs Kim. Nice to ....
2 A: Bye then, and .... for everything.
   B: Bye, Sally, ... soon.
3 A: Goodbye.
   B: Thank you for meeting us today.
   A: You're ....
   C: Have a safe journey. Thank you for ....
4 A: Hi, Leandro, ... ?
   B: Fine, thanks. And you?
   A: I'm ....

a ◯   b ◯

④ Which conversations are formal and which are informal? Practise the conversations with your partner.

c ◯   d ◯

Vocabulary ⑤ **1.11** Listen and complete the list of numbers using words in the box.

0 1 2 3 .... 5 6 7 8 .... 10 11 .... 13 14
.... 16 17 18 19 .... 21 22 23 .... 25 26
27 .... 29 30 40 50 60 70 80 90 100

More practice

⑥ Listen again and repeat the numbers.

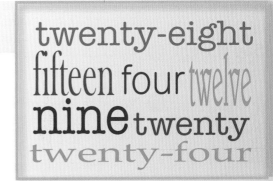
twenty-eight
fifteen four twelve
nine twenty
twenty-four

Say it right ⑦ **1.12** Practise the pronunciation of the numbers. Then listen and circle the numbers you hear.

13	30	15	50
thirteen	thirty	fifteen	fifty

⑧ **1.13** Listen and circle the number you hear.

1 19 90
2 18 80
3 17 70
4 16 60
5 15 50
6 14 40
7 13 30

Speaking ⑨ Write down ten numbers between 1 and 100. Take turns to dictate the numbers to your partner. You can check what you hear by using one of these phrases:

Sorry, I didn't get that.   Could you say that again?

Listening ⑩))) **1.14** Listen to four telephone conversations. Complete the questions.

1 What's your .... number?
2 What's the .... code for Cologne?
3 What's the .... for Mexico?
4 What's your .... ?

> **?**
> 0 = oh or zero
>
> 77 = double seven or seven seven

⑪ Listen again and write the telephone numbers.

Speaking ⑫ Ask two other people the questions from ⑩.

Vocabulary ⑬))) **1.15** Read and listen to the email addresses. Discuss the questions with a partner.

> r.juszko_05@gmail.com
>
> andrea.szabo@inco.hu
>
> swan_julia@aol.com

1 How do you say @?
2 How do you say __ ?
3 How do you say .?
4 How do you say .com?
5 Say your personal email address.
6 Say your work email address.

More practice

⑭))) **1.16** Listen and tick (✓) the email address you hear.

1 | To t.glock_9@gmail.com | a ☐ | | To t.glock_19@gmail.com | b ☐ |

2 | To l_b.roberts.8@hotmail.com | a ☐ | | To l.b.roberts.18@hotmail.com | b ☐ |

3 | To a.chau_6@yahoo.com | a ☐ | | To achau_16@yahoo.com | b ☐ |

4 | To zhang.shan@google.com | a ☐ | | To zhang_shen@google.com | b ☐ |

Speaking ⑮ Work in groups of three. Student A, look at page 97. Student B, look at page 99. Student C, look at page 101.

1 Four people want to meet at a business conference in Hong Kong. Look at the business cards of three of them. Find the information.

1 .... works in Hungary.
2 .... is Lebanese.
3 .... is the country code to telephone Beirut.

4 .... works in Barcelona.
5 .... and .... work for software companies.
6 .... is the country code for Spain.

Estrella
MULTIMEDIA

Calle San Pedro, 33, 7712 Barcelona
Tel: +34 778 990234
Email: j.fernandez@estrella.es

Javier Fernandez
Product Manager

KRYPTOSOFT

1026 Budapest, Szilagyi Erzsebet fasor 47

Agna Schmid
CREATIVE DIRECTOR

Business Systems Software
schmid.agna@kryptosoft.hu
Tel: 00 36 893 443 FAX 00 36 893 987

2  **1.17** Listen to the phone messages and complete the business card for the fourth person.

Manal Obeid
Product Consultant

IQBAL

Email: manal.obeid@Iqbal.com
Tel: (961) 1 334 556
Fax: (961) 1 645 782
100 2140 Ashrafieh Beirut - Lebanon

Name:

Company:

Job title:

Phone number:

Email:

3 Student A, read the emails below. Student B, read the emails on page 99. Complete the information in the table.

○ ○ ○

j.fernandez@estrella.es; manal.obeid@iqbal.com; schmid.agna@kryptosoft.hu

Dear all,
Look forward to seeing you tomorrow. My mobile number is 778652110. Put the country code 0086 first to call me. Let's meet in reception at 9:00.
Best wishes
Henry Wu

○ ○ ○

manal.obeid@iqbal.com; schmid.agna@kryptosoft.hu; h_wu@yahoo.com

Hi Henry,
Thanks for your number. Here's my number: 0034 777 905 6441. See you all tomorrow at 9:00.
Best wishes
Javier

Mr Wu	**Ms Schmid**
Mobile number:	Mobile number: ....
Meeting time:	Meeting time: ....
Email:	Email: ....
Mr Fernandez	**Miss Obeid**
Mobile number:	Mobile number: ....
Meeting time:	Meeting time: ....
Email:	Email: ....

4 🔊 **1.18** Three people meet in the reception area of the conference hotel. Listen to the conversation and answer the questions.

1 Who's at the meeting?
2 Who isn't at the meeting?
3 Correct any false information in the notes in **3**.

5 🔊 **1.19** Agna asks the hotel receptionist for help. Listen to their conversation. Which room is Mr Wu in? Tick (✓) the correct answer.

Room 18 ☐   Room 80 ☐

6 Work with a partner. Student A, look at the information file below. Student B, look at page 99.

You are Javier. Mr Wu comes to reception with his colleague. Speak to Mr Wu's colleague.
Greet his colleague. Find out:

INFORMATION FILE

His name

His job

Where he is from

His phone number

His email address

Say goodbye.

Work
My job

Start up

1 What are the three most common jobs in your country?

2 These are the three most common jobs in the USA.
Match the jobs a–c with the descriptions 1–3.

a salesperson

b cashier

c office clerk

1 They do many office jobs, e.g. data entry, filing, emailing and telephoning.
2 They sell products and services to customers.
3 They work at a cash register or till. They serve customers and take their money.

Vocabulary

More practice

3 Match more common jobs a–e with the descriptions 1–5.

a nurse

b waiter/waitress

c customer service representative

d truck driver

e general manager

1 They answer questions and deal with requests and complaints. Many work in call centres.
2 They work in hospitals.
3 They take orders and serve food to tables.
4 They deliver things.
5 They're in charge of a business.

4 Underline the verbs in **2** and **3**. Which ones can you use to describe your job?

Grammar

Present simple with *I, you, we, they*:

+ I/You/We/They work

- I/You/We/They don't work

>>>GRAMMAR REFERENCE PAGE 103

5 Complete the text about the waiter. Use the correct form of the verbs in the box.

earn   go   live (× 2)   not work
serve   take   work

WAITER – JOÃO ALEGRE

I ....[1] in Portugal in the capital city, Lisbon.
I ....[2] in a small apartment in the historic centre.
I ....[3] in the centre of Lisbon. I ....[4] in a restaurant in another part of town. I ....[5] people's orders and ....[6] drinks and food to the tables.
I ....[7] to work by tram and boat because the restaurant where I work is on the other side of the river.
I ....[8] €12,000 a year.

6 Complete the text about the salesman. Use the verbs in the box.

| answer | deal with | earn | go | have (x 2) | live (x 2) | not work | work |

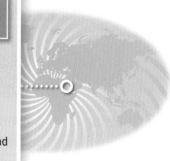

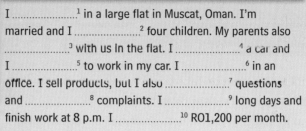

CUSTOMER SERVICE REPRESENTATIVE – ABDUL AL-FULAN

I ....[1] in a large flat in Muscat, Oman. I'm married and I ....[2] four children. My parents also ....[3] with us in the flat. I ....[4] a car and I ....[5] to work in my car. I ....[6] in an office. I sell products, but I also ....[7] questions and ....[8] complaints. I ....[9] long days and finish work at 8 p.m. I ....[10] RO1,200 per month.

7)) **2.1** Listen and check your answers to **5** and **6**.

8 Complete the sentences with the positive or negative form of the verbs in brackets.
1 In Oman, we *don't work* on Fridays because it is a religious day. (work)
2 I sometimes work in the evening, but I .... at the weekend. (work)
3 Many people .... big families because of the cost of living. (have)
4 Most people .... to work by metro in Paris because it is cheap and fast. (go)
5 Many people .... in houses because it's too expensive. Most people .... in flats. (live)

9 Read and complete the text about a hotel manager from Hong Kong. Use verbs from this page.

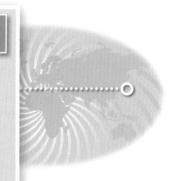

HOTEL MANAGER – KRISTY LEE

I ....[1] in a flat in Hong Kong. I'm married and I ....[2] one child. I ....[3] in a hotel in Kowloon; I'm the general manager. I ....[4] to work on the underground every day. I ....[5] normal hours every day. My hours and days are different every week.
I ....[6] one million Hong Kong dollars a year.

10)) **2.2** Listen and check your answers.

Vocabulary **11** Match words and phrases in A with phrases in B.

More practice

A		B	
1	answer	a	in an apartment / house; in Lisbon
2	be in charge of	b	in an office; normal / long hours
3	earn	c	$25,000 a year; RO1,200 per month
4	go to work	d	by tram; in my car
5	live	e	questions; the phone
6	work	f	a business; a team

Speaking **12** Work with a partner. Take turns to tell each other about your job. Talk about:
• where you live • where you work • how you go to work • what you do every day.

Start up

1 2.3 **Listen and repeat the days of the week.**

Monday	Tuesday	Wednesday	Thursday	Friday	Saturday	Sunday

2 **Which days are weekdays in your country and which are weekend days? Match the days of the weekend with the countries.**

Friday and Saturday
Saturday and Sunday

the UAE | Jordan | Germany | Qatar | the USA | Japan

Speaking

3 **Work with a partner. Take turns to ask and answer the questions.**

Which day(s) of the week do you:

- go to work?
- go out in the evening?
- go shopping?
- do sport/go to the gym?

I go to the gym on Tuesdays and Thursdays.

Say it right

4 2.4 **Listen and repeat the months and seasons.**

January	February	March	April	May	June	July
August	September	October	November	December		
spring	summer	autumn	winter			

Speaking

5 **Work with a partner. Take turns to ask and answer the questions.**

In which month(s):

- is your birthday?
- are the birthdays of your two best friends?
- do summer and winter start and finish in your country?
- do you go on holiday?

6 **Read the sentences. Check the meaning of the words in *italics*. Discuss the questions with a partner.**

1 A day when people don't work is called a *day off*. What days off do you normally have in the week and in the year?
2 Working early in the morning, in the evening and at night is called *shift work*. In which kinds of jobs do people work shifts?
3 In Europe, hotels usually have a *busy period* at New Year, Easter and in the summer. When does your work have a busy period?

?

Bank holidays or **public holidays** are days off everyone is given.

For other holidays, we say 'to take a day off'.

Listening

7 2.5 **Saud is an office manager in Riyadh, Saudi Arabia and Ali works as a night porter in Adelaide, Australia. Listen and complete the information about their working hours and holidays.**

	Saud	Ali
Days of work		
Number of holiday days		
Holiday destination		

?

night porter – someone who works nights in a hotel looking after customers and the building

Grammar

Present simple questions with *I, you, we, they*	Present simple short answers	
When do you go to work?	Do you work on Saturdays?	Yes, I do.
Where do I go for the meeting?	Do they finish at five?	No, they don't
Do they work every day?	**Have got**	
Do we start at nine?	Have you got a pen?	Yes, I have.
	Have you got a key?	No, I haven't.

>>>GRAMMAR REFERENCE PAGE 103

More practice

8 Match the elements in A with those in B and C.

A	B	C
1 How	do you work?	Yes, it's in November.
2 Where	do you travel to work?	In a hotel.
3 When	month do you like best?	Probably January.
4 Who	have a national day?	Yes, I have.
5 Which	do you live with?	My wife and children.
6 Do you	do you go on holiday?	In the summer.
7 Do you	got a car?	By car.
8 Have you	work on Sundays?	No, I don't.

9 Ask and answer the questions in **8** with a partner.

Reading

10 Read the text about working hours. Choose the best word, a, b, c or d, to complete 1–6.

1 a do	b work	c job	d are
2 a start	b do	c stop	d hour
3 a days	b minutes	c hours	d holiday
4 a people	b jobs	c workers	d countries
5 a working	b days off	c job	d hours
6 a weekend	b week	c day	d stop

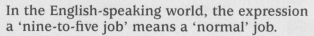

Working hours

In the English-speaking world, the expression a 'nine-to-five job' means a 'normal' job.

Many people in office jobs ....¹ from nine o'clock in the morning until five o'clock in the evening, but working hours are different across the world.

In some Southern European and South American countries, people work from eight in the morning until one o'clock in the afternoon. They ....² for lunch and then work from four until seven. But these days, many people work from nine to five because these are the working ....³ for international business.

In many countries, 48 hours a week is the maximum number of hours people can legally work, but many people work more. Many studies show that South Korea and Japan are the ....⁴ where people work the longest hours in the developed world.

In Europe and America, people work five days a week and have Saturday and Sunday as ....⁵. In the Middle East, the traditional holy day is Friday, so the traditional.........⁶ is from Thursday to Friday. This makes international business difficult, so many Middle Eastern countries now take their weekend on Friday and Saturday. ■

Speaking

11 Tell your partner about your working week. Include:
- the days you work
- your days off
- busy periods.

Start up

1 Discuss the questions with a partner.

1 What do you say when you answer the phone?
2 Is it different at home and at work?
3 Do you ever make or receive calls in English?

2 Look at the expressions for answering the phone from around the world.
Which would you use in your language? Which would sound strange or impolite?

| Hello | May your morning be good | Ready | Smith | Speak | Who's on the phone? | Who's speaking? | Yes |

3 Translate what you would say in your own language, when answering the phone, into English. Ask your teacher if you can use the same expression.

Listening

4))) **2.6** Listen to two telephone conversations. Complete the table. Use the names in the box.

| Carla Carlson | Katia | Robert Kott | Steffan | Steven Pilkington | Thomas Freund |

	Conversation 1	Conversation 2
1 the name of the person answering the phone		
2 the person making the call		
3 the person they want to speak to		

5 Listen again. Complete the conversations.

Conversation 1

Receptionist: Good afternoon, Pavilion Ltd.
Katia ....[1]. How can I help?
Carla: Good afternoon. ....[2] Steven Pilkington, please?
Receptionist: ....[3] who's calling?
Carla: ....[4] Carla Carlson.
Receptionist: One moment, please. I'll just ....[5] through.

Conversation 2

Receptionist: Good morning, Key Stage Solutions. Steffan speaking. ....[6] ?
Thomas: Can I speak to Robert Kott, please?
Receptionist: May I ask who's calling?
Thomas: It's Thomas Freund ....[7] Terco.
Receptionist: I'm sorry, he's in a meeting. ....[8] a message?
Thomas: Yes, ...[9] him to call me, please?
Receptionist: ....[10] your number?
Thomas: Yes, it's 01568 929 356.
Receptionist: Thank you. ....[11] a message for him.
Thomas: Thank you. Goodbye.
Receptionist: Goodbye.

6 Find expressions in the two conversations in **5** for each function below.

Answer the phone		Say if someone isn't there	
Ask for someone		Offer to take a message	
Ask who's calling		Take someone's number	
Say who you are			

Vocabulary

7 ·))) **2.7** Listen to how these numbers are grouped. Mark the others like the example.

00/44/60/9086
1 0049221854
2 01582587924
3 0799363921

8 Practise saying the numbers.
1 00 39 874 112
2 01289 326 859
3 965 8924
4 966 4711

9 ·))) **2.8** Listen and check.

10 Match the parts of the number with the correct word.

More practice

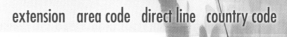

0044 (0)1284 378 7227   extension   area code   direct line   country code

11 Write the numbers and practise saying them to a partner.
1 your home phone number
2 your work number
3 your mobile number
4 your extension or direct line
5 your manager's extension or direct line
6 the country code for your country
7 the area code for your country's capital city

12 Check the numbers your partner has written down. Are they correct?

Speaking

13 Work with a partner. Use the role cards to role-play the conversation.

Student A - Mario Gomez   **Student B - Lok Wang**

Answer the phone	Ask to speak to Viviana Santi
Ask who's calling	Say who you are
The person is out. Offer to take a message	Leave your number
Thank and say goodbye	Say goodbye

Scenario: A desk of my own

① Label the picture of the office. Use the words in the boxes.

window

plant

pen

pencil

photo of my dog

coffee cup

laptop screen

chair

keyboard

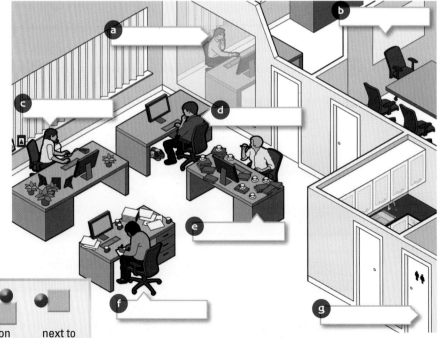

② ·))) **2.9** Listen and check.

③ Listen again and repeat the names of the objects.

④ Describe your workplace to a partner.

1 Where is your office or workspace?
2 How many people do you share an office with?
3 What furniture and equipment do you have (desk, chair, computer, etc.)?
4 What personal things do you have in your office or on your desk?
5 Is your workspace noisy or quiet? Dark or light? Big or small? Hot or cold? Is your desk tidy or untidy?

⑤ Look at the office floor plan. Read the description. Label the desks and rooms with the names in the box.

| Constantinos Emel Gizem Hazel Manos meeting room toilets |

Our office

Our office is on the second floor. Hazel is the Team Manager. She has the big desk in front of the window. It's very tidy and she has lots of plants and photos of her children. Gizem has a desk opposite Hazel. She's very untidy, so there are lots of papers on her desk and lots of coffee cups! Emel's work space is also very untidy. She drinks tea all day, so there are lots of tea cups on her desk and also English books and dictionaries. Manos' desk is also in front of the window. He runs to work every day so his running shoes are under his desk. Constantinos is the boss so he has his own office. It's on the right, next to the meeting room. On the other side of the door are the kitchen and the toilets.

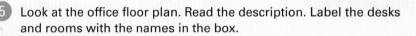

? in front of   opposite   under   on   next to

Read the email and answer the questions.

1 What's the good news?   **2** What problem is there?

> Hi Hazel,
> Brilliant news, Ana is going to start work at the company. I'm sure she's going to be a great person to work with. The only problem is that we have too many people! I want Ana to have her own desk and not everyone is full time so we need to work out who's going to share a desk. Let's meet later to discuss it.
> Constantinos

7 ⟩⟩ **2.10** Listen to a phone call between Constantinos and Hazel.
Complete the information for the three other people who work in the office.

Manos		**Gizem**		**Emel**	
Working days	....	Working days	....	Working days	....
Working hours	....	Working hours	....	Working hours	....
Out of the office	....	Out of the office	....	Out of the office	....
Meetings	....	Meetings	....	Meetings	....

8 Work in groups of three. Student A, you are Manos. Student B, you are Gizem. Student C, you are Emel. Read your notes from **7**. When do you use your desk? Complete the table.

	Monday	**Tuesday**	**Wednesday**	**Thursday**	**Friday**
a.m.					
p.m.					

9 Have a meeting to decide who can share a desk. Discuss in your group when you need the desk and why.

I need the desk on Monday.
I have a meeting on Friday afternoon so I don't need the desk.

10 Complete the email to tell Hazel about Ana's desk.

> Hazel
> We've decided that .... and .... will share a desk. Ana Dos Passos, the new employee, can have .... desk.
> With best wishes

3 A day in the life
Busy days

present simple with *he, she, it*

times

daily routines

Vera Wang
CEO,
Vera Wang Group

Start up

1 Work with a partner and answer the questions.

1 How many hours do you work each day?
2 Do you work at weekends?
3 How many emails do you get every day?
4 How many emails do you write every day?

Reading

2 Read about Vera Wang. Why does she do a lot of work in the evening?

Vera <u>does</u> a lot of her design work in her bedroom. She <u>thinks</u> about designs and <u>looks</u> at books for ideas.
She <u>finishes</u> work late. Her team sends work to her at home, and she <u>reads</u> it at night. It is the only time when lots of people don't want to speak to her.
She <u>hates</u> phones. She always tries to phone people back, but sometimes there are too many calls. She <u>asks</u> her assistant, P.J., to find out how important each call is. She doesn't use email very often. She is always available for her staff. This <u>means</u> she does a lot of different things. She <u>fixes</u> problems, <u>calms</u> unhappy clients, and <u>handles</u> unhappy employees. It's hard to be a businessperson and a creative person. She <u>organises</u> herself – everyone <u>needs</u> her for different things.

Fortune Magazine, March 16 2006 ©2006 Time Inc.

3 Read the text again. Complete the sentences.

1 She looks at ....
2 She reads work ....
3 She gets a lot of ....
4 She does a lot of ....
5 She fixes ....
6 Everyone needs her ....

Say it right

4 ◊)) **3.1** Look at the <u>underlined</u> verbs in the text and listen.

1 Which letter do these verbs end with? Which sound does each verb end with? Complete the table.
2 Listen and check. Practise saying the verbs.

1 /z/	2 /s/	3 /ɪz/
does		

5 Add the verbs to the table in **4**.

discusses   finishes   goes   plays   stops   watches

Vocabulary

More practice

6 ◊)) **3.2** Look at the clocks. Listen and repeat the times.

7 ◊)) **3.3** Listen and write the six times you hear.

a 　b 　c 　d 　e 　f

Grammar

Present simple with *he, she, it*

Use the present simple to talk about facts and things that happen regularly.

She **finishes** work late.	He **starts** work at 9.00 a.m.
BUT I / You / We / They **finish** work late.	
I / You / We / They **start** work at 9.00 a.m.	
He **doesn't finish** work late.	She **doesn't use** email very often.
Does he **finish** work late?	Yes, he **does**.
What time **does** she **finish** work?	He **finishes** work at 5.00 p.m.

>>>GRAMMAR REFERENCE PAGE 104

8 Complete the text about Carlos Ghosn.
Use the correct form of the verbs in brackets.

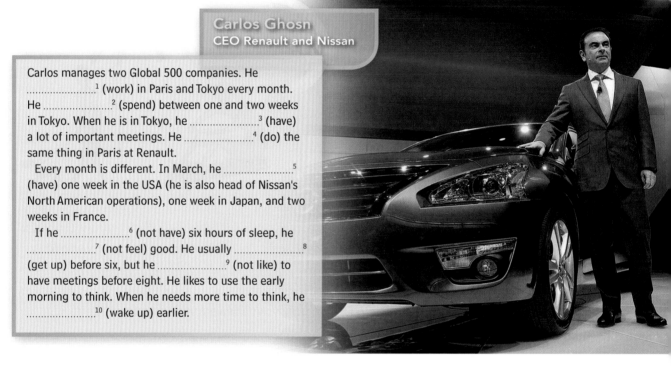

Carlos Ghosn
CEO Renault and Nissan

Carlos manages two Global 500 companies. He ....[1] (work) in Paris and Tokyo every month. He ....[2] (spend) between one and two weeks in Tokyo. When he is in Tokyo, he ....[3] (have) a lot of important meetings. He ....[4] (do) the same thing in Paris at Renault.

Every month is different. In March, he ....[5] (have) one week in the USA (he is also head of Nissan's North American operations), one week in Japan, and two weeks in France.

If he ....[6] (not have) six hours of sleep, he ....[7] (not feel) good. He usually ....[8] (get up) before six, but he ....[9] (not like) to have meetings before eight. He likes to use the early morning to think. When he needs more time to think, he ....[10] (wake up) earlier.

9 Match the questions with the answers.

More practice

1	Where does Carlos work?	a	Yes, he does.
2	Where does Vera do a lot of work?	b	Yes, she does.
3	Does Vera use email very often?	c	In Paris, Tokyo and the USA.
4	Does Carlos usually get up early?	d	No, she doesn't.
5	How much sleep does Carlos need to feel OK?	e	In her bedroom.
6	Does Vera work at home?	f	Six hours.

Speaking

10 Work with a partner and find out about their typical day. Ask questions about the activities in box 1. Use the question words in box 2.

finish work	get up	go to work	have lunch	have meetings	read email

how	what time	when	where

1 Make notes about your partner's day.
2 Tell the class about your partner's day.
Miguel usually gets up at 8.30.
3 When you listen to other students, ask some questions.
Does Miguel drink coffee?

Start up

1 Match pictures 1–14 with activities a–n.

- **a** cooking
- **b** dancing
- **c** eating out
- **d** going to the gym
- **e** playing computer games
- **f** playing football
- **g** reading
- **h** running
- **i** shopping
- **j** sunbathing
- **k** surfing the net
- **l** swimming
- **m** walking the dog
- **n** watching TV

2 Tick (✓) the activities you do. Compare your answers with a partner.

Listening

3 3.4 Listen to three people talking about their free-time activities. Tick (✓) the activities they like.

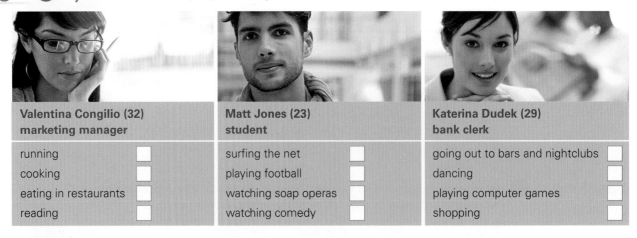

Valentina Congilio (32)
marketing manager

running	☐
cooking	☐
eating in restaurants	☐
reading	☐

Matt Jones (23)
student

surfing the net	☐
playing football	☐
watching soap operas	☐
watching comedy	☐

Katerina Dudek (29)
bank clerk

going out to bars and nightclubs	☐
dancing	☐
playing computer games	☐
shopping	☐

4 Check your answers with your partner. Make sentences.

Valentina likes running and eating in restaurants, but she doesn't like / hates cooking.

5 Listen again and answer the questions.

1. Where does Valentina work?
2. Is Valentina good at cooking?
3. What's Matt's favourite football team?
4. Why does Matt hate soap operas?
5. Where does Katerina work?
6. What does Katerina like doing at the weekend?

Grammar

> **love / like / hate / enjoy + verb + -ing or noun**
>
> I **like playing** football, but I **hate watching** football on TV.
>
> He **loves cooking**, but he doesn't **enjoy eating** out in restaurants.
>
> What does he **like doing** in his free time?
>
> I **love my job**.

››› GRAMMAR REFERENCE PAGE 104

More practice

6 Complete the sentences with the correct form of the verbs in brackets.

1 He's very active. He gets up early every day and likes .... at the gym. (work out)
2 They love .... and .... football. (run / play)
3 Her job is very stressful, so in the evening she likes .... yoga or .... swimming to help her relax. She also likes .... music. (do / go / listen to)
4 Do you enjoy .... sport on TV? What kind of sports do you enjoy .... ? (watch / play)
5 '...................... he like .... with his colleagues after work?' 'No, he doesn't drink, so he doesn't like .... to bars.' (socialise / go)

Reading

7 Read about what Vera and Carlos do in their free time. Complete the sentences.

1 .... enjoys eating with friends.
2 .... spends time with his/her children.
3 .... collects designer clothes.
4 .... doesn't read at home.
5 .... likes shopping and dancing.

Vera

Vera likes staying at home, watching television and having dinner with friends and family. She loves spending time in Palm Beach in Florida. She also enjoys visiting Shanghai – it's where her family are from originally. She loves clothes and enjoys buying other designers' clothes. She collects Prada, Yves Saint Laurent, Jil Sander, Yohji Yamamoto, Louis Vuitton and Jean Paul Gaultier. She loves going to food courts and eating food from all over the world. Vera also enjoys dancing and loves having parties at home.

Carlos

Carlos loves cars, languages, books and history. He loves spending time with his family. He travels a lot and doesn't spend much time at home. When he's at home he tries to give quality time to his wife and four children. When he's at home he doesn't read the newspaper, doesn't sit in front of his computer and he doesn't watch TV. He plays with his children and spends time with them.

Speaking

8 Interview your partner about his/her free time. Make questions from the prompts. Report back to the class.

1 What / do / you / like / do / free / time?
2 like / play / sports?
3 What kind of music / do / you / like / listen to?
4 What / do / you / hate / do at work?

Start up **1** What time do you usually have lunch? What do you eat? Where do you eat it?

Listening **2**))) **3.5** Listen to five people describe what they usually have for lunch.
Match the speakers 1–5 with the pictures of food a–f.

a ....

b ....

c ....

d ....

e ....

f ....

Say it right ③

•))) **3.6** Listen and repeat the phrases. Mark the words that are linked. Practise saying the phrases to a partner.

1 a cup of tea
2 a cup of coffee
3 a bowl of soup
4 steak and chips
5 We usually have
6 typically English

Vocabulary ④

•))) **3.7** Listen and circle the number you hear.

a 12 20 22	d 105 115 140	g 18 88 80
b 13 30 33	e 36 63 16	h 109 190 119
c 104 114 140	f 217 207 270	i 84 48 408

 More practice

⑤ Check your answers with a partner.

⑥ Practise saying the numbers.

⑦ •))) **3.8** Practise saying the prices, then listen and check.

a €10.20	e €50.15	i $5.25
b $12.50	f $66.76	j €17.87
c £15.99	g €14.40	
d £29.99	h $89	

Listening

⑧ •))) **3.9** Listen to people buying their lunches. Write the food items they choose and the prices.

⑨ Listen again. Complete the phrases for asking for food and practise saying them.

1 ....._I'd like_..... a large box of sushi.
2 .... a small soup of the day and a side salad.
3 .... a chicken sandwich, please – and a coke.
4 Two .... of vegetable curry with rice and two glasses of water.
5 .... four portions of steak and chips and four cups of tea, please.

⑩ •))) **3.10** Listen to two more people buying food and drink. Complete the conversations.

1 **Café worker:** Good morning. What can I get you?
Customer: Hi. ....ᵃ an Americano, please.
Café worker: Certainly. Regular or large?
Customer: ....ᵇ, please.
Café worker: To have here or take away?
Customer: ....ᶜ, please.
Café worker: Here you are. That's one dollar, sixty five …
    Thank you. Have a nice day.
Customer: Thank you. And you. Bye.

2 **Waiter:** Hello, madam. Are you ready to order?
Customer: Yes, please. I'll have the ....ᵈ and
    a ....ᵉ, please.
Waiter: Anything to drink with that?
Customer: Er, yes. Could I have a ....ᶠ, please?

3 **Waiter:** Anything for dessert?
Customer: I don't think so, thank you … Could I have
    ....ᵍ now, please?
Waiter: Certainly, madam.

Speaking

⑪ Work with a partner. Use the conversations to help you.
Take turns to order the items below.

1 Order what you often drink when you go to a café.
2 Order what you like to eat for lunch.

Scenario: Work or family?

1 ◄)) **3.11** When Nick arrives at his office on Thursday morning, he has a voicemail message from his boss. Listen and tick (✓) the things the boss asks him to do.

arrange a meeting for Monday	☐	read a report	☐	telephone head office	☐
take an important client out for lunch	☐	email a customer	☐	write a report	☐

2 Listen again. Complete Nick's schedule for the day.

CALENDAR | day | month | year

Mon	Tue	Wed	Thu	Fri	Sat	Sun
		1	2	3	4	5
6	7	8	9	10	11	12
13	14	15	**16**	17	18	19
20	21	22	23	24	25	26
27	28	29	30	31		

16
Thursday 16th May

○	09:00–10:00	Finish agenda for marketing meeting	9–10
○	10:00–11:00		10–11
○	11:00–12:00	Marketing meeting	11–12
○	12:00–13:00		12–13
○	13:00–14:00	Meeting with team to prepare next week's presentation	13–14
○	14:00–15:00	Finish writing the accounts report for last month (Urgent!)	14–15
○	15:00–16:00		15–16
○	16:00–17:00	Prepare my presentation for tomorrow	16–17

3 Nick needs more time to do the work for Sven. Make changes to his schedule so that he has time.

4 ◄)) **3.12** Nick phones his sister for help. Put a tick (✓) next to what he can do and a cross (✗) next to what he can't do.

Buy a present for their mum ☐
Go out on Monday night for their mum's birthday ☐

5 ◄)) **3.13** Nick takes Giancarlo to lunch in a restaurant. Listen to the first part of their conversation. What do they each order? Write Nick or Giancarlo.

.... | .... | .... | .... | ....

6 🔊 **3.14** Listen to the second part of the conversation. Nick and Giancarlo talk about what they do in their free time. Write N (Nick) or G (Giancarlo).

cooking ....   eating out ....   reading ....

cycling ....   playing tennis ....   watching TV ....

7 🔊 **3.15** Listen to the final part of the conversation. Tick (✓) the things Nick and Giancarlo have problems with.

| hot food ☐ | money ☐ | coffee ☐ | the waitress ☐ | the menu ☐ |
| cold food ☐ | credit cards ☐ | the time ☐ | the soup ☐ | |

8 There are some messages for Nick when he gets back from lunch. Complete the email with the words in the box.

| come | meet | play | says | talk |

> 〇 〇 〇
>
> To: Nick
> From: Sven
> Subject: Meeting
>
> Nick
> Giancarlo ¹...................... that lunch was bad. This is not good news.
> But I still want you to ²...................... with me on Monday evening to take Giancarlo and Luca Fellini, Giancarlo's boss, to ³...................... golf. We will also ⁴...................... about a new business opportunity – so it's important that you come. ⁵...................... us at the golf club at 6.30. Don't be late!
> Sven

9 🔊 **3.16** It's Monday. Listen to the voicemail from Nick's mother and complete the phone message.

> *Phone message*
> *To:*
> *From:*
> *Message:*
> *Don't forget* .... ¹
> *Meet her* .... ² .... ³

10 What should Nick do now?

1 Work with a partner. Student A, read the extra information on page 97. Student B, read the extra information on page 99.
2 Close your books. Tell your partner the extra information.
3 Decide together what to do.
4 You are Nick. Write a note EITHER to your mother OR to your boss to explain the situation. Use the expressions in the box to help you.

| I'm sorry, but   I'm afraid I can't come because   I have to |
| Perhaps I could / we could / could ... instead |

4 A great place to be

Around town

there is, there are
places in a city
giving directions

Start up

① Work with a partner. Where do you go to do these things? Find the places on the map.

1	catch the airport bus	*bus station*	5	buy aspirin	....
2	go for a walk	....	6	get some local information	....
3	buy stamps	....	7	get a taxi	....
4	take a client out for dinner	....	8	get some money	....

Listening

②))) **4.1** Diana is on a business trip to Rio de Janeiro. Listen to four conversations. Write where she needs to go and why.

1 Where? .... Why? ....   3 Where? .... Why? ....
2 Where? .... Why? ....   4 Where? .... Why? ....

Grammar

there is / there are

Use *there is* (*there's*) with singular nouns.

There's a post office in the town centre.

Is there a bank?   No, **there isn't** a bank, but **there's** a place where you can exchange money.

Use *there are + some* for plural nouns.

There are some excellent restaurants in this part of town.

To make questions and negative sentences, use *any*.

Are there any good bookshops near here?

No, **there aren't** any bookshops, but **there's** a good library.

>>> GRAMMAR REFERENCE PAGE 105

3 Complete the sentences.

| are there | is there (× 2) | there are (× 2) | there isn't |

1 Hi, could you tell me, ... a good restaurant near here?
2 .... lots of good restaurants.
3 .... any Mexican restaurants there?
4 I don't think .... any Mexican restaurants.
5 .... a pharmacy near here?
6 .... one near here, but there is one very near your hotel.

More practice

4 Listen to the first two conversations again and check your answers.

5 Complete the sentences with *there is* / *there are* or *is there* / *are there*.

1 .... a post office on the High Street.
2 .... a café near here?
3 .... two banks next to each other at the end of the street.
4 .... any good bars near here?
5 .... a restaurant in the hotel, but there is a good one next door.

Reading

6 Read the emails from Diana's colleagues in Rio. Answer the questions.

1 Which buildings are near their offices?
2 Who can't come to the meeting?
3 Which bar is the restaurant near?

Hi Diana,
I hope your flight is OK and you have time to relax this evening. Our meeting is at our offices in the morning. They are easy to *get / go / arrive* [1] to from your hotel. When you *leave / go / get out* [2] of your hotel, turn *left / straight* [3] and then go *straight / right / down* [4] on for two blocks until you *get / go / arrive* [5] to the traffic lights. Turn left and our offices are *on / next to / near* [6] your left *opposite / between / on* [7] the bank and the pharmacy.
See you tomorrow
Leandro

Hi Diana,
Sorry I won't be in the meeting tomorrow. For dinner in the evening, I've booked a restaurant near your hotel. Go out of your hotel and turn right, then continue straight on *until / at / when* [8] you get to the crossroads. Turn right and the restaurant is *opposite / next / with* [9] to a bar called Docas.
See you tomorrow evening
Ana

?

Directions
Turn left / right.   Go straight on.
It's opposite / next to / near …

7 Read the emails in **6** again and circle the correct option.

Speaking

8 Work with a partner. Give directions to places in your town or city. Begin like this:

Excuse me. Is there a …? Excuse me. Can you tell me how to get to the …?

Student A

1 Think of a place in your city. Tell your partner where you are in the city and where you want to go.

2 Give Student B the directions they need.

Student B

1 Give Student A the directions they need.

2 Think of a place in your city. Tell your partner where you are in the city and where you want to go.

Start up

1 Match the adjectives with the opposites in the box.

| beautiful / pretty | boring | clean | expensive | noisy |
| old-fashioned | safe | slow | small | unfriendly |

1 fast ....
2 big ....
3 dirty ....
4 dangerous ....
5 modern ....
6 friendly ....
7 interesting ....
8 quiet ....
9 cheap ....
10 ugly ....

2 Tell your partner about:

- something boring you do at work and something interesting
- an old-fashioned object or piece of technology you own or use
- a dangerous place (or person) that you know
- an exciting film or book you have seen or read recently.

Speaking

3 Work with a partner. Discuss what you know about the cities.

 Beihai
 Johannesburg
 Paris
 Tokyo

Reading

4 Read the descriptions. Write the name of each city in the highlighted space (a–d).

| big, bigger, the biggest | cheap, cheaper, the cheapest |

......................[a] is one of ....[1] cities in South Africa. The city is famous for its gold mines and because it's the home of Nelson Mandela, the former South African president. According to a recent survey, it's ....[2] city in the world for foreigners to live in, because food and housing aren't expensive.

| beautiful, more beautiful, the most beautiful | big, bigger, the biggest | small, smaller, the smallest |

Many people think that ....[b] is one of ....[3] and most romantic cities in the world and, with 30–40 million visitors a year, it's the most visited. Until the nineteenth century, this city was ....[4] in Europe, but today with a population of 2.5 million, it's ....[5] than Berlin or London.

| big, bigger, the biggest | good, better, the best |

With a population of over 13 million, ...[c] is ....[6] city in the world. It's an important global business centre. It's also one of ....[7] places in the world to go shopping or eat out. There are more top-class restaurants in this city than Paris or New York.

| fast, faster, the fastest | pretty, prettier, the prettiest |

This sea port in south-west China is ....[8] growing city in the world. With its beautiful beaches and green parks, ...[d] is ....[9] than Beijing or Shanghai and has more tourists. But it's also an important centre for trade and industry, including shipbuilding.

5 Which city/cities in ④:

1 is a port?
2 is a tourist centre?
3 has lots of good restaurants?
4 has cheap housing?
5 is a centre for the mining industry?

Grammar

Comparative and superlative

One syllable adjectives add *-er* or *-est*.

| cheap | cheaper | the cheapest |
| fast | faster | the fastest |

When the adjective finishes in a vowel and a consonant, we double the final consonant.

| big | bigger | the biggest |
| hot | hotter | the hottest |

Two syllable adjectives ending in *y* change the *y* to *i* and add *-er* or *-est*.

| easy | easier | the easiest |
| noisy | noisier | the noisiest |

Two or more syllables not ending in *y* put more or most before the adjective.

| expensive | more expensive | the most expensive |
| beautiful | more beautiful | the most beautiful |

Some adjectives are irregular.

| good | better | the best |
| bad | worse | the worst |

>>>GRAMMAR REFERENCE PAGE 105

More practice

6 Complete the descriptions in ④ with the correct form of the adjectives.

7))) 4.2 Listen and check your answers.

8 Complete the sentences with the correct form of the adjectives in brackets.

1 Paris is .... than London. (small)
2 The .... time of the day is in the evening. Everyone is out in the street talking. (noisy)
3 Life in the country is .... than life in the city. (quiet)
4 The .... part of the city is down by the river. (pretty)
5 Cities are always exciting, but for me, the .... is Barcelona. (exciting)
6 Many cities are .... than they were in the past and air pollution is .... (dirty, bad)
7 The city centre is much .... than some of the suburbs. (safe)
8 The .... university in the world is in Bologna. (old)

Speaking

9 Work with a partner and tell them about your city.

- your favourite restaurant
- where the most expensive shops/housing are
- what tourists come to visit
- the prettiest part of the city
- the busiest/noisiest part of the city

Start up

1 Match the hotel facilities with the words in the box.

air conditioning	bath	business centre	fitness centre	hairdryer
iron / ironing board	minibar	restaurant	room service	shower
swimming pool	tea- / coffee-making facilities	Wi-Fi access		

2 What is important for you when you choose a hotel? Tell your partner.

Reading

3 Complete the profiles of the three Barcelona hotels with the facilities they offer from **1**.

Situated between the airport and the conference centre, the Hotel Ronda is a modern business hotel in North Barcelona. High-speed ....[1] is free in all rooms and there is a 24-hour ....[2] for all your business needs. There are three ....[3] specialising in Italian, Chinese and traditional Spanish cuisine. To help you relax, we have a ....[4] for sport and a heated indoor pool for you to use 24 hours a day.

The Casa Sant Jordi is a family-run hotel in the city centre. All rooms have ....[5] to keep you cool and are non-smoking. There is no restaurant, but a range of drinks and snacks are in the ....[6] in each room. There is an internet café next door and lots of restaurants within walking distance.

The Mirador is a four-star hotel next to the beach. Our luxurious rooms offer a wide range of facilities including 24-hour ....[7] for snack and meals. We have one of the best spa and fitness centres in Barcelona with both an indoor and outdoor ....[8]. Our dining facilities include a French style brasserie and the main restaurant on the top floor, which is also a jazz club. Parking is available on request.

Listening

4))) **4.3** These people need to reserve a hotel room in Barcelona for three nights. Listen and complete the information.

Cristiano, charity worker

He needs a ....¹ room.

He wants to be near the ....².

Vera, executive director

She needs a hotel with ....³, ...⁴, ...⁵, ...⁶.

She wants to be near the ....⁷.

Simon, teacher, and Laura, engineer

They need a hotel with ....⁸, ...⁹, ...¹⁰.

They want to be near the ....¹¹.

5 Work with a partner. Decide which hotel in **3** is best for each of them.

Vocabulary

6))) **4.4** Listen and revise the months. Mark the word stress.

January	February	March	April	May	June
July	August	September	October	November	December

7))) **4.5** Listen and repeat the ordinal numbers.

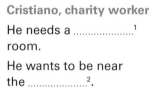
More practice

1st	2nd	3rd	4th	5th	6th	7th	8th	9th	10th	11th	12th
13th	14th	15th	16th	17th	18th	19th	20th	21st	22nd	30th	31st

8))) **4.6** Listen and write the dates you hear. Check your answers with a partner.

9 Write down five dates that are important to you. Dictate them to your partner. Why are they important?

Write:
25th June / 25 June
2nd November / 2 November

Say:
the 25th of June
the 2nd of November

Listening

10))) **4.7** Listen to Cristiano and Laura reserve their hotel rooms. Write the dates.

Cristiano	Arrival date:	Departure date: ....
Laura	Arrival date:	Departure date: ....

11 Listen again and complete the phrases.

Conversation 1
1 I'd like to make a .... for four nights.
2 I'd like a .... room.
3 Could you tell me the .... rate, please?

Conversation 2
1 Hello, I'd like to reserve a .... room for six nights.
2 Does that include .... ?
3 OK, we'll .... it.

Speaking

12 Work with a partner. Take turns to reserve a room. Student A, look at page 97, Student B, look at page 99.

Scenario: Which hotel?

1 Read the email from Colin's boss and complete his 'To do' list.

Colin,
I need you and Paula to book hotels for three important visitors we have coming. They don't need to stay in the same hotel, but they need to be near the company's office. I'll send through details of some possible hotels later, but speak to Paula now as she has the details of the clients. Bruce can be difficult, so choose his hotel well!
Oli

To do
Book hotel rooms!
Speak to
....

Possible problem
....

2))) **4.8** Colin and Paula meet to discuss the visitors. Listen and complete Colin's notes.

Visitors
1 Ayman..................... Head of Marketing
   at ....
2 .... Wang, ...
   at the Washington office
3 Bruce ....
   The new ....

3))) **4.9** Colin gets some messages from the visitors. Listen and complete the information.

Ayman hasn't got much money, so his hotel must not be ....[1]. He wants to have ....[2] in his room and he wants ....[3] to be included in the price.

For Shan, money isn't ....[4]. It must be high ....[5]. The room must be very ....[6] and she likes to ....[7] every morning so there must be a ....[8].

Bruce would like an ....[9] price hotel. It must have ....[10] stars and have excellent ....[11]. He wants a good ....[12] of the city.

4 The next morning, Colin receives some emails with extra requests from the visitors. Add to the information in ③.

Dear Colin,
Thank you for booking my room. I forgot to tell you I'm driving, so could the hotel have parking, please? When you have a hotel, could you send me some reviews so that I can check it is up to my standards.
Best wishes
Shan

Dear Colin,
Sorry, I forgot to say that I need to exercise every morning, so there needs to be a pool or a gym in the hotel. Also, I like to know before I arrive exactly how much I will spend, so please send me the costs before you book.
Kind regards
Ayman

Dear Colin,
One thing I forgot with my booking: I have to swim every morning, so please make sure there is a pool. Look forward to seeing you soon.
Best
Bruce

5 Work with a partner. Student A, read the hotel descriptions below. Student B, Look at the map and read the reviews on page 100. Decide together which hotel is best for each visitor.

World Hotel   Cost: *£250 per person per night*   Stars: 4

Facilities: All rooms come with tea- and coffee-making facilities. There is 24-hour room service available and three top restaurants. Rooms are air-conditioned and equipped with mp3 player docks, free wireless internet and flat-screen TV.

The Sherwood Hotel   Cost: *£200 per person per night*   Stars: 4

Facilities: Each room is equipped with tea- and coffee-making facilities and a minibar. Room service is available until midnight. The room comes with an internet point and there is a fully-equipped business centre for your use. There are two bars and a restaurant. The restaurant and one of the bars is on the top floor with amazing views across the city. The hotel also has a modern gym for your use.

Hathaway Hotel   Cost: *£125 per person per night*   Stars: 3

Facilities: All rooms have tea- and coffee-making facilities and a minibar. Each room also comes with a hairdryer and ironing board. The whole hotel, including each room, has wireless internet available. There is also a fully-equipped business centre. Breakfast is served each morning on the ground floor in the hotel's main restaurant.

Hotel Polo   Cost: *£75 per person per night*   Stars: 2

Facilities: Each room has tea- and coffee-making facilities. Breakfast is served each morning between 7.00 and 10.00.

6 Complete the email to one of the visitors describing the hotel you have booked for them. Try to make the choice sound very positive.

.... ,
We have booked the .... for you. It's .... hotel with ....
There .... and .... I hope you will be pleased with the choice.
Best wishes

5 Food
My diet

food
countable and uncountable nouns with *a*, *an*, *some* and *any*
describing dishes

Start up

1 Match the pictures with the different types of food.

> fast food / junk food   meat   desserts   vegetables and salad

2 Which types of food do you like? Which do you eat often? Tell your partner.

Vocabulary

3 Match the pictures with the different types of food.

More practice

> apples   bananas   beef   biscuits   carrots   cheese   chicken   chips
> chocolate   coffee   fish   ice cream   juice   mushrooms   oranges   pasta
> strawberries   tomatoes

Grammar

Countable and uncountable nouns – *a/an*, *some* and *any*

1 Countable nouns are singular or plural.

  singular: **There is** an apple, a banana, a sandwich, a carrot.

  plural: **There are** some apples, bananas, sandwiches, carrots.

2 Uncountable nouns. Use *some* and a singular verb.

  There's some bread, **some** cheese, **some** milk, **some** coffee.

  But a piece of bread / cheese, a glass of milk, a coffee (a cup of coffee) = **countable**

3 Use *any* in negatives and questions for plural countable nouns

  Are there **any** apples or bananas? There are some apples, but there aren't **any** bananas.

  and for uncountable nouns.

  Is there **any** milk? Do we have **any** cheese? No, we don't have **any** food at all.

»»GRAMMAR REFERENCE PAGE 106

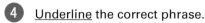

4 <u>Underline</u> the correct phrase.

1 Could you pass me *some milks* / *some milk* / *a milk*, please?

2 I don't want *any meat* / *a meat*, thank you. I'm a vegetarian.

3 Would you like *some cheese* / *a cheese* before dessert?

4 I'd like *some fish* / *some fishes* / *a fish*, please and a small green salad.

5 They don't have *any* / *some* / *an* orange juice. Would you like any apple juice instead?

6 There *is* / *are* some cheese on the table, but there isn't *some* / *any* bread.

5 Work with a partner and follow the role cards.

Student A - Mario Gomez

> 1 Write down the name of a dish.

> 2 You are allergic to fish, dairy and nuts. Your partner has invited you to their flat for dinner. Ask questions to find out if you can eat the dish they want to cook.

Student B - Lok Wang

> 1 Write down the name of a dish.

> 2 You are a vegan. Your partner has invited you to their flat for dinner. Ask questions to find out if you can eat the dish they want to cook.

Listening

6 �))) **5.1** Listen to descriptions of the dishes a–d. Number the dishes in the order you hear them.

a ◯

b ◯

c ◯

d ◯

7 Listen again. Complete the descriptions with the expressions in the box.

dessert   dish   it comes with   topped with   sauce   starter

Moussaka
It's a Greek ....¹. It's made of aubergines, lamb, tomatoes, garlic, lots of herbs and ....² cheese.

Steak
The steak is really good. ....⁴ potatoes, vegetables and a mushroom ....⁵.

Brownie
It's a ....³. It's got lots of chocolate in it.

Fish
The fish is baked in the oven and comes with salad. It's a ....⁶, not a main course.

Speaking

8 Look at the menu. Describe the dishes to your partner.

Spaghetti bolognese topped with parmesan

Fajitas with rice and beans

Sushi, made with raw fish, cucumber, rice, seaweed sheets

Fish served with a salad

More practice

Start up

1 Which countries do you associate these foods with? Are they popular in your country?

1 pizza **2** burgers **3** sushi **4** tacos **5** curry

2 Is your country's food popular around the world? Why/Why not?

Reading

3 Read the text about Gastón Acurio, a successful chef and restaurant owner. Is this statement true or false?

There are a lot of traditional Peruvian dishes on his menus.

Gastón Acurio
– The man taking Peruvian food to the world

Gastón Acurio is a Peruvian chef and restaurant owner. He owns several international restaurant franchises, has his own TV programme and cookery school in Lima and is also the writer of many cookery books.

SO WHY IS HE SO SUCCESSFUL?

Gastón's cooking style is a mix of European cooking with traditional South American ingredients. For example, there are a lot of delicious root vegetables from the time of the Incas that grow in the Andes, such as the arracacha, the mashua, the maca, and the yacon. He uses these in many of his dishes. He also uses the leaves of the coca plant, llama and guinea pig meat and a lot of seafood. With his German wife and business partner, Astrid, he helped to start a whole new style of cooking called la Cocina NovaAndina or 'new Andes cooking'.

But Gaston Acurio is not only an excellent cook; he is also a man with a vision. He wants to make Peruvian food popular around the world. His four main restaurant franchises are:

Astrid & Gastón HIGH-QUALITY 'GOURMET' RESTAURANTS

Tata INFORMAL FAMILY RESTAURANTS

la mar CEBICHERIAS OR PERUVIAN-STYLE SEAFOOD RESTAURANTS

Pasquale SANDWICH SHOPS

Gastón Acurio wants to take Peruvian food and Peruvian cooking and make them into global brands. From Peruvian cooking, he plans to build global food brands with as much power as Japanese sushi, Mexican tacos or Italian pizza.

SO WATCH OUT!

A Peruvian style sandwich bar or a cebicheria could open near you very soon.

4 Read the text again. Answer the questions.

1 Which country is Gastón Acurio from?
2 Who is Astrid?
3 What is special and different about Gastón Acurio's food?
4 Find the names of four of his international restaurant chains.
5 What is La Cocina NovaAndina?

Vocabulary

More practice

5 Complete the sentences with the correct form of the words highlighted in green.

1 Potatoes and carrots are common .... in Europe.
2 A .... gives someone the right to sell a product using the company's name, for example, Starbucks™ and McDonald's®.
3 Corsica is between France and Italy and its food is a .... of French and Italian food.
4 The best restaurants use good quality ....
5 The letter M is the .... of a famous American fast food restaurant.
6 Famous chefs have the .... to make people choose different foods.

Grammar

6 Look at the words in the text highlighted in yellow and complete the Grammar box with *countable* or *uncountable*.

---

much, many* and *a lot of

1 How **many** restaurants does Gastón have?

He doesn't have **many** cookery schools. He has one.

Use *many* for negatives and questions with .... nouns.

We can also use *many* in positive sentences.

He is the writer of **many** cookery books.

2 How **much** seafood is there?

Gastón is very busy – he doesn't have **much** time.

Use *much* for negatives and questions with .... nouns.

Don't use *much* in positive sentences.

~~He has much time. There is much cheese.~~

3 Gastón owns **a lot of** restaurants and he makes **a lot of** money.

Use *a lot of* for positive sentences with both .... and .... nouns.

>>>GRAMMAR REFERENCE PAGE 106

7 Complete the sentences with *much, many* or *a lot of*.

1 There are .... Mexican restaurants around the world.
2 There's .... fish and rice in Japanese cooking.
3 Pizzas don't have .... meat on top.
4 There aren't .... foods you can't find in London.
5 We have to take .... customers and partners out to lunch.
6 How .... coffee did you drink this morning?

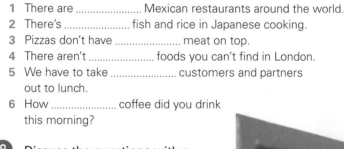

More practice

Speaking

8 Discuss the questions with a partner.

1 Why do you think many people want to own a restaurant or café?
2 Would you like to own a restaurant? Why/Why not?
3 Would you like your own business? Why/Why not?

Start up **1** Imagine you have visitors to take for dinner from a different country. What do you know about table manners in other countries? Choose which option you think is correct for each country.

Different behaviour is polite in different countries. For example, in Japan *it's / it isn't*[1] normal to pick up a bowl of soup and bring it to your mouth. In America, people hold their fork in their *right / left*[2] hand. In the UK, *it's / it isn't*[3] polite to keep your elbows on the table, but in France it *is / isn't*[4] polite to do the same thing. In Saudi Arabia, people eat with their *left / right*[5] hand. In El Salvador, you *should / shouldn't*[6] leave a little food on the plate. In South Korea, talking *is / isn't*[7] common during a meal.

2 ◀)) **5.2** Listen and check your answers.

3 What other ways can you be polite in your country during dinner?

(?)

Opinions and offers
Say *I like* to give your opinion on something, for example: *I like fish.* = I enjoy eating fish.

Say *I would like* when you want something, for example: *I would like some fish.* = I want to eat some fish and not, for example, some meat.

Listening **4** Complete each conversation with *Would you like / Do you like* or *I like / I'd like*.

1	.... a coffee?	No, thanks. I don't drink coffee.
2	.... spicy food?	Yes. I love it!
3	.... a slice of cake?	Yes, please.
4	Can I help you?	Yes, ... a table for two, please.
5	How's your dessert?	Good! .... cake, especially chocolate cake.

5 ◀)) **5.3** Listen and check. Practise the conversations with a partner.

Say it right **6** Match the questions and responses.

1	Could we have a table for four, please?	a	No thanks, I'm full.
2	Would you like some more rice?	b	White, with two sugars, please.
3	Could you pass the water, please?	c	Still or sparkling?
4	How would you like your coffee?	d	Certainly, is this one OK?
5	Shall we split the bill?	e	Of course. Here you are.
6	Could I have a glass of water, please?	f	No, it's my treat.

7))) **5.4** Listen and check your answers.

8))) **5.5** Listen and repeat. Notice how the intonation goes up to show politeness. Practise saying the phrases with a partner.

Could we have a table for four, please?

Small talk is informal conversation about general topics that are not serious or important

Listening

9 Tick (✓) the topics that you think are good for small talk with someone you don't know very well.

☐ politics ☐ food ☐ weather ☐ religion ☐ sports ☐ family

10))) **5.6** Listen to the conversations. What topics do they discuss?

11 Match the question or statement with the response.

1	It's so cold!	a	Me too.
2	How often do you play?	b	She's a doctor.
3	It's not normally this bad.	c	I usually go shopping and sometimes eat out.
4	What does your wife do?	d	It's freezing, isn't it?
5	So, is this a traditional dish?	e	I hope not!
6	I love swimming.	f	Yes, it's one of the most popular dishes in the country.
7	What do you do at the weekend?	g	Once or twice a week.

Speaking

12 Often when we reply we use a synonym to repeat what the person said. Match the synonyms.

It's so cold!   *It's freezing, isn't it?*

1	amazing	a	boiling
2	hot	b	dull
3	boring	c	wonderful
4	exciting	d	tasty
5	delicious	e	fun

13 Work with a partner. Take turns to give an opinion on a topic in **9** using words from **12**.

Pepe e Sale

HOME   MENU   CONTACT

Pepe e Sale is a local Italian restaurant which specialises in traditional Italian cooking. Our pizzas are baked in a traditional oven and are the best in town. This family-run business is owned and managed by Salvatore Morretti. There is a real family feel to the restaurant with much of the Morretti family working there. The restaurant is great for a quiet intimate night or for big parties with seating for up to 40 people.

1 Read the text and complete the table.

Name of restaurant	
Type of cooking	
Owner	
Maximum number of customers	

2 ·))) **5.7** Listen to people eating in the restaurant. Make notes about the strengths and weaknesses of the restaurant.

Strengths	Weaknesses

3 ·))) **5.8** Listen to Salvatore and the consultant talking about the business. Complete the table.

Number of years open	
Total debt	
Number of staff	
Staff wages per week	
Rent and bills	
Cost of ingredients per week	
Number of customers per day	
Average spend per customer	

4 Work with a partner. You find two reviews of the restaurant online. Student A, read the review below. Student B, read the review on page 101.

	Review A	Review B
Decoration		
Food		
Service		
Waiters		

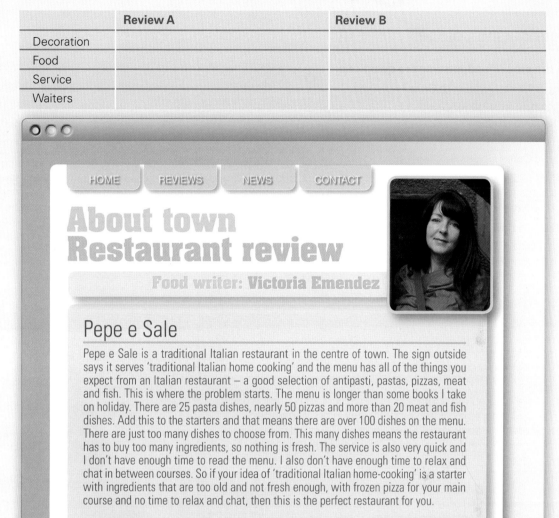

HOME   REVIEWS   NEWS   CONTACT

About town Restaurant review

Food writer: Victoria Emendez

Pepe e Sale

Pepe e Sale is a traditional Italian restaurant in the centre of town. The sign outside says it serves 'traditional Italian home cooking' and the menu has all of the things you expect from an Italian restaurant – a good selection of antipasti, pastas, pizzas, meat and fish. This is where the problem starts. The menu is longer than some books I take on holiday. There are 25 pasta dishes, nearly 50 pizzas and more than 20 meat and fish dishes. Add this to the starters and that means there are over 100 dishes on the menu. There are just too many dishes to choose from. This many dishes means the restaurant has to buy too many ingredients, so nothing is fresh. The service is also very quick and I don't have enough time to read the menu. I also don't have enough time to relax and chat in between courses. So if your idea of 'traditional Italian home-cooking' is a starter with ingredients that are too old and not fresh enough, with frozen pizza for your main course and no time to relax and chat, then this is the perfect restaurant for you.

5 Tell your partner the problems you found and complete the table.

6 Produce one list of problems. Put the problems in order from most important to least important.

7 Write an email to Salvatore of your findings. Tell him what the main problems are and make suggestions for how he could improve the business.

Writing emails

1 Introducing yourself

Read the emails and answer the questions.

1 Why is Montse writing to David?
  a to apply for a job in Madrid
  b to offer David work
  c to ask about possible work

2 Who is Daniel Rojas?
  a a manager in the UK
  b a manager in Madrid
  c a temporary* IT worker

3 When will David email Montse again?
  a in October
  b next month
  c immediately

*temporary = only for a short time

To: david.martin@opchem.com
From: montse.cabral@gmail.com
Subject: work experience?

Dear David
My name is Montse Cabral. I'm working on a six-month contract for your company in Madrid. Daniel Rojas, the head of IT here, gave me your name. I'm 22 years old, and I'm a graduate in computer science.
I want to go to the UK in October for six to twelve months to work and to improve my English.
I'm writing to ask if there are any positions in your company. My CV is attached.
I look forward to hearing from you.
Montse Cabral

To: montse.cabral@gmail.com
From: david.martin@opchem.com
Subject: Re: work experience?

Hi Montse
Yes, Daniel emailed me about you. Nice to meet you! There are sometimes opportunities for temporary staff in our department. At the moment, I don't know about October. There's a planning meeting next month, so I'll contact you immediately after that.
Best wishes
David

To: david.martin@opchem.com
From: montse.cabral@gmail.com
Subject: Re: work experience?

Thanks, David

Focus on ... the greeting

Dear David	formal
Hi David / Hello David	neutral / informal
Hi / Hello	informal OR when you don't know the name of the person
[no greeting]	very informal; used after the first email of a conversation
Dear all	neutral / formal, writing to a group
Hi all	informal, writing to a group
Dear Sir/Madam	very formal; used when you don't know the person's name

Style tip

Use abbreviated forms in your emails to make them sound more natural:

I am ⟶ I'm   do not ⟶ don't
There is ⟶ There's   I will ⟶ I'll

Language tip

Notice that we use different prepositions after *work*.
to work **on** a temporary contract / a project
to work **for** a company
to work **in** IT

Task

You want work or work experience. Use the notes to write an email introducing yourself to tanya.nording@opchem.com in the UK. Use expressions from this page or from the Phrasebank to help you.

- subject line
- polite greeting
- your name
- current work
- got Tanya's name from manager, Wili Holst
- your qualifications / experience / speciality
- your plan: one year in UK (for experience and language)
- reason for writing: work / work experience opportunities?
- CV attached
- polite ending and signoff

2 Leaving an out-of-office message

Read the emails. Complete the sentences using the names in the box.

> Rino   Elena   Stefano   Fabienne

1 .... is a freelance photographer.
2 .... is managing the brochure project.
3 .... works in the same office as Elena.
4 .... is designing the brochure.

From: fabienne.lafarge@gmail.com
To: egalbiati@spiroeditorial.com
Subject: Soderberg cover photos

Hi Elena
I've uploaded the cover photos for Stefano to your FTP folder. Let me know if there's a problem.
Best
Fabienne

From: egalbiati@spiroeditorial.com
To: fabienne.lafarge@gmail.com
Subject: out of office

I am out of the office until Wednesday, September 2, and will reply to your message when I return. If it is urgent, please contact my colleague Rino Conti at rconti@spiroeditorial.com.
Elena Galbiati

From: fabienne.lafarge@gmail.com
To: rconti@spiroeditorial.com
Cc: egalbiati@spiroeditorial.com
Subject: cover photos for Stefano Sirimarco

Hello Rino
I'm working with Elena on the Soderberg brochure. She asked me to upload some cover photos today, but she is out of the office. Could you pass my message on to the designer, Stefano Sirimarco, please?
Thanks
Fabienne

Focus on ... out-of-office messages

This is an automatic reply you can switch on in your email program when you are away, and cannot answer messages personally.

Points to remember:

- Keep it short and simple.
- Make it formal, because you don't know who will read it.
- Don't be creative – use the standard expressions.
- You can leave contact information in case someone's message is urgent – tell your contact person about this.
- Remember to switch off the automatic reply when you return!

Style tip

When you ask someone to do something in an email, writing *please* and *thanks* make your email sound polite:
If it is urgent, please contact my colleague ...
Could you pass my message on to the designer, please?
Please send me the link.
It is common to use *Thanks* as a signoff:
Thanks
Fabienne

Language tip

Note the prepositions used with future dates:
I will be away from my desk ...
on *27 February.*
until/till *2 March.*
from *27 February to 2 March.*
between *27 February and 2 March.*

Task

You're going on holiday tomorrow for two weeks. Use the notes to write an out-of-office message. Use expressions from this page or from the Phrasebank to help you.

- return: 7 September
- will reply: 7 September
- urgent? message on +34 (0)7777-777777
- OR email > jose.tierra@blencoe.com (colleague)

3 Sending and replying to an invitation

Read the emails. Match each question with a name or names.

Who ...

1	can come to dinner?	Luis
2	will be at the airport?	Maria
3	has to leave without eating?	Tanya
4	sends the most formal reply?	Pierre

○ ○ ○

From: Jaume Busquets (busquetsj@cattmark.com)
To: tanya.weiss@weissgrafix.com, pierre.hetier@schaffers.be,
luis.delossantos@pikapika.es, maria.pereira@imprimat.com
Subject: Invitation to dinner

Dear all
We would like to invite you to dinner with the rest of the team at the Jade Garden restaurant on Thursday 3 July at 7.30 for 8. The restaurant is near the railway station, about 10 minutes' walk from the conference centre. Please could you let me know by Friday 20 June if you will be able to attend.
Jaume

○ ○ ○

From: tanya.weiss@weissgrafix.com
To: Jaume Busquets (busquetsj@cattmark.com)
Subject: Re: invitation to dinner

Thanks, Jaume. I'd love to come.
See you at the conference.
Tanya

○ ○ ○

From: pierre.hetier@schaffers.be
To: Jaume Busquets (busquetsj@cattmark.com)
Subject: Re: invitation to dinner

Hi Jaume
I'm afraid I can't make it to dinner, but will come for a drink and to say hello at 7.30.
Best
Pierre

○ ○ ○

From: luis.delossantos@pikapika.es
To: Jaume Busquets (busquetsj@cattmark.com)
Subject: Re: invitation to dinner

Dear Jaume
I will be able to attend. Thank you for the invitation.
Best wishes
Luis

○ ○ ○

From: maria.pereira@imprimat.com
To: Jaume Busquets (busquetsj@cattmark.com)
Subject: Re: invitation to dinner

I'd love to come, but my flight leaves at 10. Thanks for the invitation, though. See you all at the conference.
Maria

Focus on	... the signoff
David	neutral / informal: be careful, as this can seem cold or unfriendly if you don't know the person well
Best wishes	neutral
Regards	neutral
Yours	formal
Best	informal
Cheers	very informal
D	(= just first letter of name); very informal and friendly

Style tip

Note that invitations are usually sent to a number of people, and so are often more formal than the reply. For example:
Please let me know if you are able to attend the meeting.
could be answered formally if you don't know the sender:
I will be able to attend the meeting.
or informally if you know them personally:
Thanks – I can come to the meeting.

Language tip

When you say no to an invitation, it's best to say it in a gentle way. Here are some phrases which make your reply softer:
I'd love to come, but unfortunately *I'll be away on that date.*
I'm afraid *I won't be able to come because I am at a conference that day.*

Task

1 You're having an office party. Use the notes to write an informal email inviting your freelance colleague polly.davidson@gmail.com to the party. Use expressions from this page or from the Phrasebank to help you.

- subject line
- friendly greeting
- party: 7 June, 5–8 p.m.
- venue
- invite
- request reply
- friendly ending and signoff

2 You've received the following invitation:

Subject: workshop invitation

We would like to invite you to a workshop on 3 May from 10 a.m. to 12.30 p.m. Please let me know if you can attend.
Yours
Amy Kennedy

Use the notes to reply to the invitation. Use expressions from this page or from the Phrasebank to help you.

- polite greeting
- accept OR say no to the invitation
- polite ending and signoff

4 Giving directions

Read the emails and look at the map.
Is the restaurant at A, B or C?

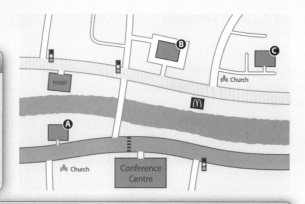

From: tanya.weiss@weissgrafix.com
To: Jaume Busquets (busquetsj@cattmark.com)
Subject: Re: Invitation to dinner

Jaume, can you tell me how to get to the Jade Garden, please?
I can't find it on the internet.
T

From: jaume.busquets (busquetsj@cattmark.com)
To: tanya.weiss@weissgrafix.com
Cc: pierre.hetier@schaffers.be, luis.delossantos@pikapika.es, maria.pereira@imprimat.com

Dear all
Tanya tells me it's hard to find the Jade Garden on the internet, so here are some directions:
It's about ten minutes' walk from the conference centre. If you're walking from there, you turn left out of the main entrance. Cross the main road at the crossing, then go across the bridge and turn right, then take the second turning on the left. The Jade Garden is about 50 metres along on the right, down a little sidestreet. It's got a big tiger outside it – you can't miss it*.
If you're staying at the Four Seasons Hotel, it takes about five minutes. Turn right out of the hotel, and go straight on at the traffic lights. When you get to McDonald's, you'll see a church on the other side of the road. Go down the sidestreet next to it, and the restaurant is the second entrance on the left.
See you there. Call me if you get lost! (+44 (0)7777 777777)
Jaume

*You can't miss it
= It's very easy to see

Focus on   ... recipients

To

Next to 'To', you put the address(es) of the person or people you are sending the message to.

Cc

If you want to send a person a copy of an email you are sending, you use 'Cc'. For example, if you send an email to another team member, it could be useful to 'copy in' the team leader.

Bcc

If you want to send a copy to someone without other recipients knowing, use 'Bcc'. This means 'blind carbon copy'.

Groups

If you send an email to a number of people, you can make a 'group' in your email program, and send the email to the group. This is useful if you do not want everyone to see all addresses.

Style tip

When people send an informal email, they often end with a friendly comment, such as:
Speak soon.
See you there / next week.
Have a good weekend.
Hope the trip/presentation, etc. goes well.
Looking forward to seeing you.

Language tip

The most usual ways to give instructions are to use the 'imperative' (= the verb without *you*) or the present simple:
Turn *left at the lights.*
You turn *left at the lights.*

Task

A colleague, Léonie Blanc, needs to come to your house from her office in the centre of town.
Use the notes to email her instructions how to get there on foot from the nearest public transport. Use expressions from this page or from the Phrasebank to help you.

- friendly greeting
- directions
- reason for writing
- friendly ending and signoff

5 Saying what you need

Read the emails and decide if sentences 1–5 are true or false.

1 The restaurant manager has already spoken to Jaume.
2 Jaume would like snacks with the apéritif.
3 The group would prefer to sit inside the restaurant.
4 The cost will be £31.50 per person.
5 Jaume orders the same food for everyone.

○ ○ ○

From: jaume.busquets (busquetsj@cattmark.com)
To: info@thejadegarden.com
Subject: Cattmark group booking

Hello
As we discussed on the phone, we'll need a table for 15 people at 8. We'll arrive at 7.30 for drinks. We'll order drinks from the bar, but if you could put out some nibbles, that would be great. Could we have outside tables, if possible, please? We'd like to have the taster menu for everyone, at £35 per head, not including group discount. We need two with vegetarian options.
Thanks
Jaume Busquets
Sales Manager
Cattmark Engineering

○ ○ ○

From: info@thejadegarden.com
To: jaume.busquets (busquetsj@cattmark.com)
Subject: Re: Cattmark group booking

Dear Mr Busquets
It was good to speak to you earlier. That's fine – we have reserved the outside terrace for your group. The discount will be 10%.
We look forward to seeing you.
Vincent Wong
Manager
Jade Garden Restaurant

Focus on **... following up an earlier conversation**

If your email follows an earlier phone call or email, start by saying this:

As we discussed on the phone, ...
As I mentioned this morning, ...
As promised, I'm sending you our brochure.

Style tip

There are several ways to start an email in a friendly way if you know the person.

neutral	**informal**
It was good to talk to you on the phone.	*It's good to hear from you!*
I hope everything is going well.	*How are things (with you)?*

Language tip

You can say what you need in several ways.
Some can sound more strong and formal, and some less.

stronger ↑
We need the files by Friday.
We'll need the files by Friday.
Can you send the files by Friday, please?
Could you send the files by Friday, please?
If you could send the files by Friday, that would be great.

Task

You're at a conference in another country. You are organising lunch out for a group of ten people at a local restaurant. Write an email to bookings@starofindia.com. Use the notes to tell the restaurant what you need. Use expressions from this page or from the Phrasebank to help you.

- greeting
- book private room (discussed it on phone)
- details:
  - 1 p.m. (order immediately); finish by 2.30 (important)
  - 'taster' menu ($25/head)
  - 3 vegetarians
  - water (still and sparkling); no wine
- thanks
- friendly ending and signoff

6 Arranging to meet

Read the emails and decide if sentences 1–4 are true or false.

1 Jeff and Taro are going to talk business in the afternoon.
2 They are going to meet at 6 o'clock.
3 They are going to eat at Fagin's.
4 Taro is going to call Al-Salam.

From: Jeff Blumberg
To: Taro Ishikawa
Cc: Charles Dove
Subject: meetup?

Hi Taro
I'm arriving the day before the conference, in the afternoon. It would be good to meet up, and maybe have dinner later. I thought we could meet at Fagin's at around 5 to catch up and run through the presentation over coffee. Then in the evening we could maybe get together with Charlie and the rest of the team and go and eat somewhere. If you're happy with that, what time would suit you? And where shall we eat?
Jeff

From: Taro Ishikawa
To: Jeff Blumberg
Subject: Re: meetup?

Hi Jeff
Good idea. An hour later would suit me at the café. How about eating at Al-Salam about 8? I know it's expensive, but it's your turn to pay ;). BTW, bring lots of business cards.
Taro

From: Jeff Blumberg
To: Taro Ishikawa
Subject: Re: meetup?

LOL -- I knew you would remember! ☺ That's good for me. I'll call Charlie, and book the restaurant.
J

Focus on ... abbreviations

It is best not to use abbreviations in business emails. The other person may not understand them, or they may be too informal. Some abbreviations that you may see in a business email are:

ASAP as soon as possible
FYI for your information

Style tip

It can be risky to use humour in emails, because the recipient can't hear your tone of voice or see your face. Emoticons and abbreviations are a way to show that you are joking, or that you understand the other person's joke:

;) (winking and smiling) = I'm joking
XD (closed eyes and a big smile) = that's very funny!
LOL ('laugh out loud') = that's very funny!

Language tip

There are several different ways for making suggestions. Some are stronger than others:

We could (maybe) go to Luigi's.
I thought we could go to Luigi's.
How about (going to) Luigi's?
Shall we go to Luigi's?
I suggest we go to Luigi's.
Let's go to Luigi's.

stronger ↓

Task

You will be near your friend Charlie Walker's office tomorrow. Use the notes to email him to arrange to meet up. Use expressions from this page or from the Phrasebank to help you.

- friendly greeting
- reason for writing (near office; would be good to meet up)
- coffee
- Plaza Hotel
- what time?
- friendly ending and signoff

**Tick (✓) the abilities and experience which are mentioned in
the job ad and in Ines's email.**

Ability / Experience	mentioned in job ad	mentioned in email
can use main software		
experience as manager		
finishes work on time		
good leader		
university degree		
previous work on magazine		
talented		
web design experience		

New high-quality Travel magazine seeks
brilliant graphic designer
experienced in managing a team.

You must be able to provide top-quality work to a deadline, and inspire others to do the same. Send CV with the names of two referees, plus two examples of your work, to margot.leonard@trex.com

○ ○ ○

From: Ines Delgado (inesdelgadosanchez@gmail.com)
To: margot.leonard@trex.com
Subject: Application for post of graphic designer

Dear Ms Leonard
I am writing to apply for the post of graphic designer, as advertised on graphjobs.com. I am a 23-year-old Spanish national, and I have an MA in Graphic Design from the Barcelona Design Institute. I have six months' experience working for a leading sports magazine, where I was in charge of a small team of designers. At the moment, I am working for a local newspaper, where I design and manage the content of the website. I have experience working with all the main design programs. I believe I have the qualities and experience necessary for the position.
My CV is attached, together with some pdfs of my magazine and newspaper work.
Thank you for considering* my application. Please contact me if you need further information.
I look forward to hearing from you.
Ines Delgado

*considering = looking at and thinking about

Focus on ... including attachments

If you include attachments, mention it in the email.
formal
Please find my CV attached.
Please find attached a sample of my work and a completed form.
neutral
My CV is attached.
I have attached my CV.
Of course, don't forget to attach the document(s)!
But if you do forget, you can resend the email, saying:
Sorry, I forgot to attach the document(s).

Style tip

Job applications have their own style of language. **It's safest not to be creative** when writing an application email – just **use standard phrases** such as the ones included here, and make sure you include all the information that the employer asks for.

Language tip

In a job application, you usually say what you are doing at the moment, and what the parts of that job are. Notice how you use **present continuous** and **present simple** to do this:
*At the moment, **I am working** for a local newspaper, where **I design** and **manage** the content of the website.*
*At the moment, **I am working** in a department store, where **I serve** customers and **deal with** money.*

Task

You have seen a job ad on the acme.com website for a job in an English-speaking country. The job seems perfect for your qualifications and experience, and it is a great company to work for. Use the notes to write a job application to humanresources@acme.com. Use expressions from this page or from the Phrasebank to help you.

- greeting
- reason for writing (including where you saw the ad)
- age / nationality / qualifications
- relevant experience, including managing team
- why you are the right person for the job
- attachments
- appropriate ending and signoff

8 Reporting conversations

Read the emails. What was Marian Behr's opinion of the marketing plan? Match the beginnings and endings of the sentences.

1 The television commercial	**a** was unsuccessful before.
2 The internet plan	**b** was too expensive.
3 The social networking idea	**c** was excellent.
4 The advertisement in a newspaper	**d** was good.

From: Fatima Rebek (fatimar@dkt.com)
To: Jens Nordgren (nordgrenj@dkt.com)
Subject: today's meeting

Sorry I missed this morning's meeting – my train was delayed by an hour! Was Marian Behr there? What did she think of our marketing plan?
Fatima Rebek
Assistant Marketing Manager
DKT Solutions

From: Jens Nordgren (nordgrenj@dkt.com)
To: Fatima Rebek (fatimar@dkt.com)
Subject: today's meeting

No worries about missing the meeting. Yes, Marian gave us her opinion of the plan.
Unfortunately, she didn't think it was very good overall. She said the idea for a TV ad cost too much, and she told us to concentrate more on web marketing instead. She thought the Facebook plan was great, but she didn't like the newspaper ad idea, because it didn't get good results last time.
She asked us to have another think and send her a new plan in a week.
She suggested we speak to Marin Blazek in New York for advice.
So, let's talk about it tomorrow.
J
Jens Nordgren
Marketing Manager
DKT Solutions

Focus on ... signature

If you work for a company, your emails may automatically include your name, title and name of company under your message. If you do not work for a company, you can add a signature in your email program. It is useful to include:

- title and/or qualifications
- job title or profession
- contact telephone number

For example:

Dr Miodrag Ćirić MSc PhD
Freelance Systems Analyst
00000000000 / 0777777777777

Style tip

It is OK not to put your name at the end of an email if you are emailing a close colleague, but it can seem rude if you don't know the person well. Using just your initial could seem too friendly.

Language tip

When you express a negative opinion, it's usual to make *do/did* negative, for example:
She didn't think it was very good.
I don't think it's their best product.
~~She thought it wasn't very good.~~
~~I think it's not their best product.~~

Task

You're going to make a presentation at a conference with your colleague, Becky Schwarz. You have just shown the presentation to two marketing managers, Tony and Marisa, at your company to get their opinion, but Becky was not at the meeting. You received this email from Becky.

Use the notes to reply to Becky. Use expressions from this page or from the Phrasebank to help you.

- greeting
- missed meeting – no problem!
- Tony and Marisa – presentation generally good
- details:

Sorry I missed the meeting – I was ill yesterday. What did Tony and Marisa think of the presentation?
B

Tony	Marisa
too long	make it simpler
check statistics	more visuals
great visuals	funny!

Read the emails. Tick (✓) the things that Soren and Ravi *have* to do.

send in work in less than a week	
work quickly	
include suggestions for library photos	
send only original content	
send text from their own site	
meet tomorrow	

From: Soren Kristensen (soren@galaktika.com)
To: Ravi Virdee (ravi@galaktika.com)
Subject: Fwd: Re: In-Medicine site

So, what's the news on the In-Medicine website?
What do we have to do, and when do we have to do it by?
S

From: Ravi Virdee (ravi@galaktika.com)
To: Soren Kristensen (soren@galaktika.com)
Subject: details for In-Medicine site

We have to send in the website content by the end of the month. That's in 10 days, so we mustn't waste any time. We can include suggestions for library photos if we want to, but we don't have to. She said all the content must be original – that's really important. So we can't use those great articles from our own site, unfortunately! The website has to go live in 3 weeks' time, so we have to do a really good job of this.
Let's meet up tomorrow morning or Monday and talk about this.
Ravi

Focus on ... keeping the inbox easy to search

Sometimes, there can be a lot of emails in one 'conversation'. If people just press 'Reply' every time, all the subject lines will begin with 'Re:...'. This makes it difficult to find information in the emails later, so it is best to give your email a **new subject line** after a few emails.

When you **forward** an email to another person, check the subject line makes the email easy to find in their inbox. For example, 'Fwd: Re: Contract' would not make an inbox search easy; changing the subject line to 'Fwd: Marie's comments on contract' would be more useful.

Style tip

You must sounds too strong in English:
~~You must finish by 8 May.~~

Here are some softer ways to say this:
We have to finish by 8 May.
It has to be finished by 8 May.
The deadline is 8 May.

Language tip

That is used in writing to refer to the previous phrase. It is especially useful in emails, as it avoids repeating words, and keeps the message short.
We have to finish by 8 May – that's in two weeks' time.
Martha thinks the price is too high, but that's just <u>her</u> opinion.
$3,000? That's ridiculous!

This is used to refer to the general topic we are discussing, not just the previous phrase.
This is an important project.
We can discuss this tomorrow.

Task

You and your colleague, Sam McCall, have a new task of writing a report on a sales conference.
Use the notes to email Sam details about the project. Use expressions from this page or from the Phrasebank to help you.

- friendly greeting
- project: report on sales conference
- deadline: Friday (3 days!)
- important!: include reports on all presentations
- include photos (if good)
- important!: don't include negative customer comments!
- important to work quickly
- speak on phone tomorrow?
- signoff

10 Making suggestions

Read the emails and decide if sentences 1–6 are true or false.

Alessandra thinks ...

1 the product's name is too small.
2 the photo should be lower.
3 the colours need to be brighter.
4 the writing on the back of the box should be bigger.
5 the photo of the woman with the product needs to be higher.
6 the number of boxes needed may change.

From: thomas.brille@protronix.com
To: alessandra.pelosi@protronix.com
Subject: F650 box pdf

Alessandra
Attached is a pdf of the box design for the F650 phone. We look forward to receiving your feedback.
Yours
Thomas

From: alessandra.pelosi@protronix.com
To: thomas.brille@protronix.com
Subject: Re: F650 box pdf

Hi Thomas
Overall, I really like the design. However, we have some suggestions for changes which we feel will improve it.
First, I really like what you've done with the name of the product, but I think it needs more space. Maybe you could move the photo of the phone down a little, which would leave more room. Secondly, we don't think the colours are right on the photo – they are a little too bright. It might be a good idea to ask the photographer to send you the original file.
Finally, we think the small print on the back of the box needs some work. It's not quite big enough to read, we think – I suggest you use the same size font as on the lid. To make more space for this, how about moving the photo of the woman with the phone up a little? As you know, we need twenty boxes for Monday's trade fair. Before printing the boxes, it might be worth double-checking the quantity with David.
Thanks
Alessandra

Focus on ... reading before you send

When sending an email, it's important to read the email through before you click 'send'. Here is a checklist to make sure that your emails look professional:

Check the 'tone'. Never send an **angry** email – this can be bad for your relationship with the recipient. Check that you have a **friendly greeting and signoff**, plus a **friendly sentence** at the start and/or end of your email.

Check your English. If you are not sure of a phrase, type it into an internet search engine in double quotes (" "). If it is a correct, standard email phrase, it should get 100,000 or more 'hits'. If it has fewer, check your phrase. Also, use the **spell-checker** in your email program, but don't depend on it 100%, because it won't understand the difference between *their/there, too/two, by/buy*, etc.

Check that you have included the basic elements of your email: Are the **recipients** correct? Is the **subject line** helpful? Have you included the necessary **attachments**?

Style tip

When commenting on someone's work or performance, it is good practice to start with a positive comment, even if your overall opinion is negative. This helps to maintain a good relationship, and motivates the recipient to want to continue working with you! Here are some phrases you can use:
Overall, I really like the design / your idea, etc.
Your suggestions/points were very interesting.
I thought many of your ideas were excellent.
Your idea/proposal certainly gives us a good starting point.

Language tip

We often need to use adjectives when giving constructive criticism. Here are some ways to do this in a gentle way:
*The colours are a **little too** bright.*
*The design is **not quite** original **enough**.*
*The instructions could be **a little** clearer / **a little less** complicated.*

Task

Your colleague, Giulia Vincenzi, asked for your comments on a PowerPoint presentation she will give at a conference. Use the notes to email her your comments. Use expressions from this page or from the Phrasebank to help you.

- greeting
- purpose of email
- positive comment

- suggestions:
  - visual at start not interesting – change?
  - graphs and charts – fewer?
  - product description – too complicated!
  - too long

- rewrite and send me script?
- friendly ending and signoff

Phrasebank

1 Introducing yourself

I'm a 24-year-old graduate in Marketing.
I'm 24, and I'm a Marketing graduate.
I have a degree in Economics from the University of Salamanca.
I have an Economics degree from Salamanca University.
I have a Masters degree in Graphic Design.

Your current activity

I'm a sales representative for a software company.
I'm working as a designer for a magazine.
I work for Enichem. (= long-term job)
I am working in a clothing factory. (= temporary job)
I'm planning to go to the USA.
I'm completing my Masters degree in Business Studies.

Your reason for writing

I'm working with you on the project.
I'm writing to ask you if there are any opportunities for work experience.
I'm writing to ask you if there may be any work experience opportunities next year.

How you know the person

Agnethe Svensson gave me your name.
Agnethe Svensson put me in touch with you.

2 Leaving an out-of-office message

Thank you for your message / email.

I'm away from my desk ...
I will be away ...

from ... to/until ...
I will return on ...

I will not have access to my email.
I will have limited access to my email.

I will reply to your email/message when I return.
I'll get back to you then.

If the issue is urgent, ...
If your message is urgent, ...

If you need to contact me urgently, ...
If you are emailing about conference bookings, ...

... please contact my colleague John Gardner (john.gardner@acme.com, +44 (0)7777-777777)
... please email the department administrator Marie Leven (marie.leven@acme.com)
... you can reach me on +44 (0)7777-777777

3 Sending and replying to an invitation

Inviting

We would like to invite you to dinner / a party / a workshop ...
on 3 June / June 3 / June 3rd / 3rd June
at 7 / at 7 o'clock / at 7 p.m. / from 7 p.m. to 11 p.m.

neutral / informal	formal
We're having a party / a training day for the sales team on 16 April...	
...and it would be great if you could come.	...and we would be very pleased if you could attend

Requesting a reply

neutral / informal	formal
	Please let me know if you will be able to / can attend
Let me know if you can come.	will be attending by 21 May

Accepting

neutral / informal	formal
I'll be there!	I will be able to attend.
I'd / I would love to come.	I would be delighted to
Thanks! / Thanks for the invitation.	attend.

Saying no

neutral / informal	formal
I'm afraid I can't come.	
I'm afraid I can't make it.	Unfortunately, I will not be
I won't be able to make it, I'm afraid.	able to attend.
I can't make that day, unfortunately.	

Giving a reason

I'd love to come, but I'm flying / I'm in Paris / I'll be on leave that day.
I'm afraid I won't be able to come, as I'll be in Madrid.

4 Giving directions

Instructions

Turn/Go left/right
Turn left into High Street / rue de Rivoli
Take the first turning on the left
Take the second on the right
Go straight on
Cross/Go across the road
Go up/down the road

Where

at the (traffic) lights
at the second set of (traffic) lights
at the end of the road
when you see a tall building
just past the police station
when you get to the end of the road/a crossroads ...

it's on the left/right
it's straight in front of you
it's straight ahead of you
it's next to a supermarket
it's opposite KFC

you'll see it on your right
you can't miss it

5 Saying what you need

We need the files by Friday.
I need you to send the files by Friday.
We'll need the files by Friday.
Can you send the files by Friday, please?
Could you send the files by Friday, please?
If you could send the files by Friday, **that would be** great.

6 Arranging to meet

Inviting

We could (maybe) go to Luigi's.
I thought we could go to Luigi's.
How about (go**ing** to) Luigi's?
Shall we go to Luigi's?
I suggest we go to Luigi's.
Let's go to Luigi's.

Where

Where would you like to meet?
Where do you want to meet?
Where shall we meet?

When

What time would suit you?
When's good for you?

7 Applying for a job

Dear Sir/Madam

I would like to apply for the post of ... advertised in ...

I am finishing my degree in ...
My degree was in ...

At the moment, I am working/studying ...

I believe I have the necessary qualities ...

I am enthusiastic.
I am very hard-working.
I work very hard at everything I do.

Please find attached my CV and application form.

I have attached some examples of my work.
I hope my application is of interest to you.
My CV is attached. / I have attached my CV.

If you would like further information, please contact me.
I look forward to hearing from you.

8 Reporting conversations

What was the outcome?
What happened?
What did she say about the proposal?

What did he think of our offer?
Let me know.

She told us to think about it.
He asked us to make a few changes.

9 Explaining deadlines

We have to finish by 8 May.
It has to be finished by 8 May.
The deadline is 8 May.
That's in 10 days, so we mustn't waste any time.
We can ... if we want to, but we don't have to.
All the content <u>must</u> be original – that's really important.

10 Making suggestions

Maybe you/we could make it larger.
It might be a good idea to make it larger.
Perhaps you/we should make it larger.
Could you/we make it larger?
Would it be possible to make it larger?
Do you think you/we could make it larger?
Why don't /we make it larger?

I suggest you/we make it larger.
I suggest mak**ing** it larger.

6 Getting around

It's quicker to walk

present continuous
travel

Start up

1 **Match the words with the photos.**

bike	bus	car	plane	scooter	train	underground/subway

2 **Which forms of transport do you use?**

Listening

3 **6.1 Listen and write how each person travels to work.**

Juan .... Ann .... Omar .... Da Long ....

4 **Listen again. Complete the information about how they travel to work.**

1 Juan can .... a car and a scooter. He doesn't like .... to work, so he .... the bus.
2 Ann .... her scooter to work. She doesn't like the busy roads and thinks it's quicker going .... scooter.
3 Omar can't .... the underground because his city doesn't have one. He doesn't .... the bus because it's too slow. He goes .... car.
4 Da Long doesn't .... the bus because it's too slow. He .... the underground.

5 **Choose the best words to complete the questions.**

1 How often do you go to work *by/on* foot?
2 How often do you travel *by/on* train?
3 How often do you *drive/ride* a car?
4 How often do you *take/drive* a taxi home?
5 How often do you *ride/take* the underground?
6 How often do you *drive/ride* a bike to work?

> ?
> How often do you ...?
> every day
> once a week
> twice a month
> three times a week
> never

6 **Ask and answer the questions in 5 with a partner.**

Reading

⑦ Read the text and complete the sentences.

Juan	Ann	Omar	Da Long
'I'm working from home this week. I have some important deadlines to meet and it's easier for me to concentrate at home.'	'The trains aren't running this week. The train company are on strike so I'm taking my car.'	'My colleague's giving me a lift to work this week. My car's at the garage.'	'I'm working in our Lisbon office for six weeks so I'm staying in a hotel. I'm actually taking the boat to work every morning! I'm staying in the old town and the offices are on the other side of the river.'

1 .... and .... are not working in their normal office this week.
2 .... doesn't like working in the office when he has an important deadline.
3 .... normally drives to work.
4 .... likes to take the train more than the car.
5 .... doesn't live in Lisbon but is working there now.
6 .... is driving to work this week.

> **?**
>
> **give someone a lift**
> – when you take someone somewhere
>
> **get a lift**
> – when someone drives you somewhere

Listening

⑧)))) **6.2** Listen to three people and answer the questions.

	Juan	Ann	Omar
Why are they late?			
What's happening at the moment?			

Grammar

Present continuous		
I'm (am) + verb + *ing*	*She/He/It's (is)* + verb + *ing*	*We/They're (are)* + verb + *ing*
Describes temporary activities		Describes activities happening now
They aren't taking the train this morning.		She/He's waiting for a bus.
Are you cycling to work today?		He's sitting in a traffic jam.

>>> GRAMMAR REFERENCE PAGE 107

⑨ Complete the sentences. Use the correct form of the verbs in brackets.

1 Normally I .... (finish) work at 6.00, but this week I .... (work) until 7.00.
2 I usually .... (walk), but today I .... (take) the bus because it .... (rain).
3 I always .... (stay) at the airport hotel before flying.
4 The underground is never late. It always .... (leave) on time.
5 I .... (work) today. I've got a day's holiday.
6 My wife .... (check) her emails all the time. She .... (sit) in an internet café now because our connection at home isn't working.

 More practice

Speaking

⑩ Write down four things you normally do every week in your job and things you are only doing this week. Tell your partner.

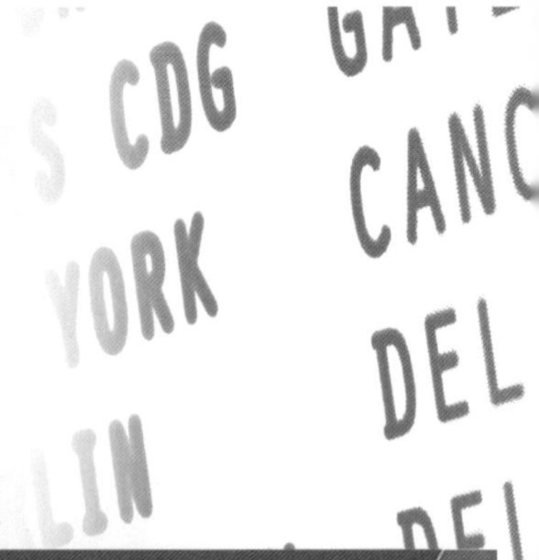

Start up

1 Read the tips about reducing travel stress. Tell your partner which ones you do and which you think are a good idea.

1 Write a checklist of things you need to take.
2 Don't worry about delays – you can't control them anyway.
3 Pack as early as possible.
4 Eat a good, healthy meal before a long journey.
5 Get to the airport at least three hours before your scheduled flight.

Listening

2 6.3 Listen to Larry. Draw his route on the map.

Reading

3 Read Larry's email and answer the questions.

1 Which places is he flying to?
2 Which places is he driving to?
3 In which city is he staying in the Sheraton?
4 Where does he still need to book a hotel?
5 When's he flying home?

Dear all,
All my flights and hotels are now confirmed so here is my latest schedule. I fly into Dubai at 7 p.m. on 8th March and have a one-hour wait before I fly on to Jeddah. I'm staying in the Sheraton Hotel for two nights. I don't need collecting from the airport – I'm taking a taxi and checking into the hotel late. On the morning of the 10th, I fly out of Jeddah at 9 a.m. and I arrive at the hotel in Riyadh at 10.30. I'm staying at the Hilton for 4 days. For the rest of the trip I'm renting a car. I'm driving to Dammam on the 14th and staying at the Ramada. I leave Dammam on the 16th and I'm driving to Bahrain. I need to book a hotel for Bahrain, but I'm planning to stay at the InterContinental.
I fly home on the 20th.
Look forward to meeting you all next week.
Best wishes
Larry

Grammar

Present continuous – future arrangements

Use the present continuous (*be* + verb + *ing*) to talk about future arrangements.

I'm flying on the Friday because I get quite bad jet lag.

We're travelling with BA on the 11 o'clock flight.

Are you staying at the InterContinental in Manama next week?

>>> GRAMMAR REFERENCE PAGE 107

4 Decide if the sentences refer to the present (P) or the future (F). <u>Underline</u> the words that help you to decide.

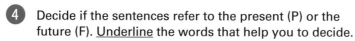

1 George's flying to Shanghai on Sunday.
2 This week, they're working in a different office.
3 What are you doing tomorrow? Can you help me with my presentation?
4 She isn't working today – it's her day off.
5 I'm having lunch with Andrea later.
6 At the moment, I'm writing a report on travel.

More practice

5 Work with a partner and make arrangements to meet. Student A, look at your travel plans on page 97. Student B, look at your travels plans on page 101.

Vocabulary

6 Use the words and phrases in the box to complete sentences 1–6. You might need to change the tense of some verbs.

| arrive / leave | book a hotel / flight | check in (for a flight / to a hotel) |
| need a visa | rent a car | take a taxi |

More practice

1 I can't .... to my hotel until 2.00 p.m.
2 My parents aren't .... They don't like driving on the left.
3 My flight .... at 10.00 on Tuesday morning and my return flight .... at 10.00 p.m. the same day.
4 In the European Union, you don't .... to travel to other EU countries.
5 I'm not catching a bus – it's very slow. I'm .... to the airport. It costs more, but it's quicker.
6 You should .... soon. There's a conference that week and the hotels will be busy.

Say it right

7 The word *is* (and *'s*) is only a separate syllable after words ending in *s*, *se*, *ge* and *ch*. Look at the examples and decide if *is* and *'s* are a separate syllable or joined to the previous one.

1 She's working in London next week.
   Joined to the previous syllable
2 The bus is leaving at 10 o'clock.
   Separate syllable
3 My flight's leaving at 8 o'clock.
4 George's flying to Shanghai on Sunday.
5 I'm moving rooms. The noise is awful.
6 Paris is wonderful.

8))) **6.4** Listen and check.

Speaking

9 Discuss your plans for the weekend with a partner. Ask and answer questions.

What are you doing on Saturday morning?   *I'm going shopping with my daughter.*

Where are you going?   *To the city centre.*

Start up ① Do the words relate to travelling by train or travelling by plane?
Write them in the correct column.

carriage	check-in desk	day return ticket
departure gate	flight number	
gate number	hand luggage	
overhead locker	platform	season ticket

Travel by train	Travel by plane

② Label the plane.

| aisle seat | exit row | window seat | wing |

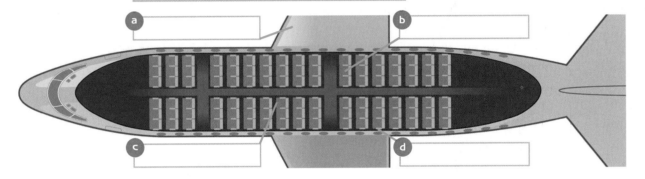

a _____
b _____
c _____
d _____

Speaking At the airport

③ You arrive at the airport. What do you do next? Label each stage with the words in the
box and put them in the correct order.

board the plane	check your gate number	check in your luggage
find the check-in desk	get a boarding pass	go through passport control
go to the departure lounge	go to your gate	

Listening

4))) **6.5** Listen to two conversations. Where are the people?
Write the number of the conversation next to the location.

check-in desk ☐   departure lounge ☐   arrivals hall ☐

5 Put the phrases from the conversations in the correct order.

Check-in assistant:	No, that's fine. How many bags do you have?	☐
Passenger:	Could I have an aisle seat?	☐
Check-in assistant:	Certainly.	☐
Check-in assistant:	Can I have your passport, please?	☐
Passenger:	Just one.	☐
Check-in assistant:	Could you put it on the scales for me? Thanks.	☐
Passenger:	Here you are. Do you need my booking reference?	☐

Tourist:	I need to go the Hilton Hotel.	☐
Tourist information:	Around $50. The underground is only $6.	☐
Tourist information:	Around 25 minutes.	☐
Tourist:	Great, thank you.	☐
Tourist information:	Yes madam. How can I help?	☐
Tourist information:	You could take the subway, the bus or a taxi.	☐
Tourist:	How long does it take?	☐
Tourist:	How much is a taxi?	☐

6 Listen again and check.

7 Practise the conversations in **5** with a partner.

At the station

8))) **6.6** Listen to the first part of three conversations. Where are they going?

9 Match the passenger phrases with the ticket officer responses.

Passenger	Ticket officer
1 What time does the 14.15 arrive?	a Platform 4, but there's a 45-minute delay.
2 Could I get a ticket for that train, please?	b Sure. Single or return?
3 Excuse me, can you tell me which platform the 12.05 to Naples departs from?	c How would you like to pay?
4 Could I have a single to Brussels, please?	d The 14.15 gets in at 15.15.
5 By card, please.	e Would you like a receipt?
6 Yes, please. Which platform is it?	f The 12.05 will now depart from platform 12.

10))) **6.7** Listen and check your answers.

Speaking

11 Work with a partner. Choose a role card each and practise the conversation using phrases from **5** and **8**.

Card A - passenger

You want to know:
The time of the next train to Paris
How much it costs
The platform it goes from
You would like a return ticket and a receipt

Card B - ticket officer

The next Paris train leaves at 11.27
It costs 75 euros return
It goes from platform 7

1 Richmond Café is an international group of cafés. Read the email from Marek (the head of the Polish market) to Magda (the Katowice manager) and Rosie (the Marketing manager, who's based in Warsaw). Complete the list about what is happening and what they need to organise.

Richmond

1 The café .... very well.
2 The team need to ....
3 Marek wants them to ....

> ○ ○ ○
>
> Dear Magda and Rosie,
> I hope you're all well. I'm writing to you all to express my concerns about the Richmond Café in Katowice. I'm sure you all know we are not reaching our sales targets. The Richmond group always adapts to local needs so we need to find out why we are not performing well. Do we need to change our product range? Do we need to improve our advertising? Do we need to change the design of the café?
> I think the best thing is for us to all arrange a meeting in Katowice. The Marketing team are working hard, but I'm sure you can find some time, Rosie. Magda: I'm sure you're doing an excellent job, so don't worry – new locations are always difficult.
> Kind regards
> Marek

2 Read the emails suggesting times and dates to meet. Choose the correct verb form.

> ○ ○ ○
>
> Dear Marek and Rosie,
> I just thought I should let you know some of my schedule for next week. I can't meet on Wednesdays because our stock *arrives / is arriving*[1] then every week. Monday is not great as the assistant manager *takes / is taking*[2] a holiday. I also can't make Friday morning as we *interview / are interviewing*[3] new staff then.
> See you soon.
> Best wishes
> Magda

> ○ ○ ○
>
> Dear Marek and Magda,
> Monday is also not good for me as *I meet / I'm meeting*[4] Dieter (the Germany manager) then. *I stay / I'm staying*[5] in Berlin until Monday evening, but Wednesday is not good as *I visit / I'm visiting*[6] a possible new location. Fridays are also not good as we always *plan / are planning*[7] the following week's visits then.
> Best regards
> Rosie

3 Discuss with a partner what days are good for Rosie and Magda.

4 Write an email from Marek explaining what days are possible for a meeting. Use the information below.

Monday: meeting in Milan
Wednesday: meeting in Milan
Friday: holiday

5 ᴐ))) **6.8** Listen to a conversation between Marek and Rosie. When do they decide to meet?

6 Read the email and complete it with the phrases in the box. What options do they now have?

| Perhaps | Really sorry, but I'm afraid | Why don't we |

Hi both,

......................[1] I'm going to have to reschedule our meeting. There are strikes on Tuesday at the airports from 10. I'm arriving at 9.00 so I can get to Warsaw, but not on to Katowice. ....[2] try taking the train and meeting later on Tuesday? Or ....[3] meeting Thursday might be better. I think we'll need at least three hours for our meeting.
Let me know what you think.
Best wishes
Marek

7 Look at the travel timetables. When is the best time for them to meet?

TUESDAY	
WARSAW – KATOWICE TRAINS	
DEPARTS: 10.00	ARRIVES: 12.30
DEPARTS: 11.15	ARRIVES: 14.45
DEPARTS: 14.15	ARRIVES: 17.45

THURSDAY ○ **MILAN WARSAW FLIGHTS**

MILAN WARSAW FLIGHTS:

DEPARTS: 7.30	ARRIVES: 9.30
DEPARTS: 8.30	ARRIVES: 10.30
DEPARTS: 9.30	ARRIVES: 11.30

WARSAW – KATOWICE FLIGHTS	
DEPARTS: 9.45	ARRIVES: 10.45
DEPARTS: 11.00	ARRIVES: 12.00
DEPARTS: 13.45	ARRIVES: 14.45

8 Write an email from Marek to Magda and Rosie suggesting the best time(s) to meet.

9 Exchange your email with a partner and write a reply confirming the departure and arrival times. Also include information about when and where to meet.

Start up

1 Match the phrases with the photos.

> apply for a job   be promoted   graduate from university
> study at school   study at university   work as an intern

2 Complete any of the sentences you can to make them true for you.

1 I studied .... in my final year at school.
2 I .... a degree. I graduated from university in .... I studied .... at university.
3 I trained in a company as a ....
4 I worked as an intern at ....
5 I was promoted in .... to ....
6 I applied for my first job in ....

3 Tell your partner about the true sentences for you.

Reading

4 Read the text. What company is it describing and what do they sell?

Family business

Stefan Persson was born in 1947. His father, Erling, lived in Sweden and was the son of a butcher. Erling travelled to New York just after World War II and really liked the big department stores there, like Macy's. So when he returned to Sweden he opened a store called Hennes ('Hers' in Swedish). The shop offered cheap but stylish clothes, just like it does today. When the first store opened in Stockholm, people queued for a long time to get into the shop.

The company changed its name to the world famous H&M in 1968 after buying Mauritz Widforss. At the same time, Stefan studied at Stockholm University and worked for the company.

He graduated in 1973 and then helped the company get bigger abroad. In 1982, the company promoted him to CEO. By 1985, there were 200 stores across Europe, by 2007, 1,300 stores in 24 countries and, by 2012, 2,500 stores in 43 countries. It didn't open its first US store until 2000, but now it has over 200 shops. Today it sells stylish clothes from top designers and still at cheap prices.

It's amazing how a family's situation can change so much in 65 years – his grandfather was a butcher, then his father opened a clothes shop in Sweden. But in 2012, *Forbes* magazine placed Stefan in the top ten richest people in the world, worth $26 billion.

5 Read the text again and answer the questions.

1 What did Stefan's grandfather do?
2 Why did his father open Hennes?
3 When did Stefan finish university?
4 How many H&M shops were there in 2007?
5 In 2012, how many countries were H&M in?
6 How much was Stefan worth in 2012?

Grammar

More practice

Past simple – *be* and regular verbs	
Use the past simple to talk about completed past actions.	
Positive	
I/He/She/It **was**	You/We/They **were**
All other forms of the past simple are the same for all pronouns.	
Regular past verbs end in *-ed*.	finish**ed**, work**ed**
Negative	
Use *didn't* + infinitive (without *to*).	
I/He/She/It/We/You/They didn't finish school.	

»» GRAMMAR REFERENCE PAGE 108

6 Complete the text with the past simple of the verbs in brackets.

MIUCCIA PRADA

Miuccia Prada ....[1] (be) born in 1949 in Milan. Her family ....[2] (be) rich. Her father ....[3] (manage) a company and her mother's family ....[4] (own) a business that ....[5] (produce) luxury products. She ....[6] (study) Politics at Milan University and ....[7] (graduate) in 1973. She then ....[8] (train) to be a mime artist for five years.

She ....[9] (study) fashion, and quickly ....[10] (become) very successful in her family's business. In 1978, when she ....[11] (start) to work for the family business, there ....[12] (be) only two shops. She ....[13] (add) many new products such as shoes and perfume. The 1990s ....[14] (be) very successful for Prada and in 2005, *Time* magazine ....[15] (name) her as one of the 100 most influential people in the world for her influence on the fashion industry. In 2012, *Forbes* magazine said that at nearly $7 billion, she ....[16] (be) in the top 150 richest people in the world.

Say it right

7 7.1 Listen to how these three regular past forms are pronounced. Write them in the table.

stopped lived wanted

1 /ɪd/	2 /t/	3 /d/

8 Add the words to the table in **7**.

awarded developed finished graduated liked managed
produced started studied trained worked

9 7.2 Listen and check.

Speaking

10 Complete the sentences with *did*, *was* or *were*.

1 Where .... you born?
2 .... you like school?
3 What subjects .... you study at school?
4 What .... you study after school?
5 .... you do an internship?
6 What .... your father's job?

11 Ask and answer the questions in **10** with a partner.

Start up

1 Look at the photos. Which place do you like shopping in?

2 Tick (✓) the sentences that describe your attitude to shopping.

1 I'm happy to pay a high price for quality.
2 I like to get a good deal.
3 I try to get things for free.
4 I'm careful with my money.
5 I don't care what I spend.

3 Show your answers to a partner and discuss your reasons why.

Reading

4 Read the text and match the headings with the paragraphs.

1 Giving things away   2 Getting a good deal   3 Living on nothing

Everything is free

a _____

Mark Boyle didn't spend any money for a year. He didn't buy any food or clothes. He didn't drive anywhere.
How did he do it? Well, he grew his own food, he got his clothes from bins and he only took phone calls and didn't make them. Why did he do it? The Irish born Economics graduate thinks we need to change how we shop and live for the environment. However, are companies and technology changing it for us anyway?

b _____

King Gillette, the founder of the razor company, only sold 51 razors and 168 blades in the first year of his business. Over the next two decades, he gave away or sold razors cheaply wherever he could. The razors were useless without the blade, so using this strategy he created a market for his razor blades. This model is now one that many companies follow. Companies gave away the cell phone and sold the minutes, printers became cheaper and ink became more expensive.

c _____

The web made even more things become free. Free music, free newspapers, nearly everything Google offers is free. And when it's not free, it helps us find a bargain. Companies like Groupon, created by Andrew Mason, and others like Livingsocial, offer discount vouchers for people to buy. When Nordstrom Rack offered $50 of clothes for $25 dollars on Groupon, over 600,000 people bought the voucher. While we might not be prepared to get our clothes from a bin like Mark Boyle, it seems we all like a good deal.

5 Read the text again. Are the sentences true or false?

1 Mark Boyle drove to work.
2 Mark Boyle made lots of phone calls.
3 King Gillette gave away lots of blades.
4 Many companies do the same as Gillette.
5 Andrew Mason created Livingsocial.
6 The Nordstorm Rack deal was popular.

Vocabulary

More practice

6 Match the nouns in the box with the correct verb.
Some can go with more than one verb.

a restaurant	breakfast	clothes	coffee
coke	dinner	friends	lunch	money
shopping	the bill	the bus	the metro
time	town

1 go
2 pay
3 drink
4 eat
5 buy
6 try on
7 pay for
8 have
9 leave
10 meet
11 spend
12 take

7 Work with a partner. Try to add two more nouns to each verb in **6**.

Grammar

Past simple – irregular verbs	
Many verbs in English have an irregular past form. get – got, have – had, do – did, go – went	
Negatives Use *didn't* + infinitive	I didn't go shopping.
Questions Use *did* + infinitive without *to*.	When did you go?

More practice

››› GRAMMAR REFERENCE PAGE 108

8 Work with a partner. What is the past simple of the verbs in **6**?

Listening

9 ·)) 7.3 Listen to Anna and Marc talking about their weekend.
Write the name under the things each person did.

Speaking

10 Work with a partner and find out what they did at the weekend.
Tick (✓) the verbs as you use them. Try to use as many as possible.

| buy | do | drink | drive | eat | go | have | meet | spend | take |

Start up

① Look at the pictures. When did you last receive/buy a gift from/for a visitor? Tell your partner what gift you bought or received and why.

Reading

② Read the text below and decide which country it is best to take gifts to.

GIFTS AROUND THE WORLD

I had an international visitor last week. As usual I got something from the storeroom to give as a gift. It was just a pen with the company logo on it. The visitor gave me a really good quality designer pen, gift-wrapped beautifully. I was so embarrassed!

Imagine you go to see an international partner. Do you buy them a present? They invite you round for dinner at their house. Do you take them something? Does it matter that the answer is no to both these questions? Well, it depends where you go.

In Mexico, people don't usually give gifts in a first meeting. When you want to give something, make it small, such as something from your company with the company logo. When a Mexican colleague invites you to their house, it's a good idea to take flowers, chocolates or wine. Gifts are opened immediately.

In India, you can take gifts to a first meeting, but it's not important to. There are many religions in India, so don't take some presents like wine or leather goods. It's a good idea to wrap presents in green, yellow or red because they're lucky colours. Gifts are usually opened later.

In Japan, gifts are an important part of business. They're a sign of friendship and respect. The gift doesn't need to be expensive, but should be of good quality. In a group, give the gift to the person with the highest status or give a gift to everyone. Don't wrap it in white, as white is linked to death. Give the gift with two hands and give it at the end of the meeting.

③ Read the text again and answer the questions.

1 When should flowers, chocolates or wine be given as gifts in Mexico?
2 Why should you not take wine as a gift in India?
3 Are gifts opened immediately in India?
4 Can you give a cheap gift in Japan?
5 What colour paper shouldn't you wrap a gift in for a Japanese person?

④ Discuss the questions with a partner.

1 Are there any presents people shouldn't give in your country?
2 Are there any colours that are bad luck?

Listening

5 Look at the pictures and the store guide. Which floor are they on?

2	Men's clothes
	Home entertainment and electrical goods
	Toys and games
	Restaurant
1	Women's clothes
	Shoes
	Children's clothes
G	Jewellery
	Perfumes and cosmetics
	Stationery
	Bags
B	Food hall
	Home appliances

a

b

6 ◀))) **7.4** Listen to three people in the store. Which floor do they need to go to?

1 Martha needs the .... floor.
2 Luca needs the .... floor.
3 Da Long needs the .... floor.

7 ◀))) **7.5** Listen to the rest of Da Long's conversation and tick (✓) what he buys.

pen ☐   bag ☐   perfume ☐

c

d

8 Match the questions and answers.

1	Do you need any help?	a	Yes, that's all thanks.
2	Can I have one of those, please?	b	Which floor are bags on?
3	How many would you like?	c	Certainly, is there anything else?
4	Is that everything?	d	Yes, but not American Express.
5	Do you take credit cards?	e	I'll take four, please.
6	Which floor is that on?	f	It's on the top floor.

9 Listen again and check.

Speaking

10 Work with a partner and look at the role cards below.

Student A

1 Go to the department store and buy:
   • a business-card holder   • some shoes.
2 You work in the department store. Look at the information and serve the customer.
   • The necklace costs $75.   • Books are on the first floor.

Student B

1 You work in the department store. Look at the information and serve the customer.
   • The card holder costs $15.   • Shoes are on the second floor.
2 Go to the department store and buy:
   • a necklace   • a book.

1 Work with a partner. Look at the pictures and discuss the questions.

1 When did you last buy any of these things?

2 Where did you buy them?

3 Do you always buy them from the same place?

2 Christina and Paul want to start a business selling only British food. They are trying to decide between a shop and an online business. What advantages and disadvantages do you think there might be to each?

	Advantages	Disadvantages
Online		
Shop		

3 After doing some research, they find out the following information. Work with a partner and choose the best type of business for Christina and Paul.

Last year	Store	Online business
Average number of customers per week	1,000	700
Average each customer spent per week	£50	£80
The cost of rent per week	£500	£200
The bills and salaries per week	£2,000	£1,500
Products	£30,000	£30,000
Delivery costs per week	–	£600

4 Discuss with a partner why you think the store got more customers last year than the website, but the website customers spent more money.

5))) **7.6** Christina and Paul speak to some people about where they shop. Listen and tick (✓) where they shop.

1 online ☐ store ☐

2 online ☐ store ☐

3 online ☐ online ☐
store ☐ store ☐

6 Listen again and match a reason with a person in **5**.

a Likes to see, feel and look at the product.
b Likes to get food delivered.
c Only shops when needed.
d Easy to buy everything.

7 Think about the customer comments and the costs again. Write a list of reasons for and against each and make a final decision. Use past simple verbs.

Last year, each customer spent more online.
Some customers preferred to see the products.

8 Make a final decision and share your reasons with a partner.

8 Getting it right
Getting it wrong

past simple – negative forms
failure

Start up

1 Look at the pictures and discuss with a partner what mistakes you think they made.

2 Complete the sentences about yourself and then discuss them with a partner.

- The last thing I forgot was ....
- I didn't remember ....
- I lost ....
- The last mistake I made was ....

Reading

3 Dal LaMagna is a multi-millionaire American entrepreneur. Read the texts below about some of his businesses. Are the sentences true or false?

1 Dal didn't have the money to start the holiday dance.
2 Computer dating is a modern idea.
3 The movie was made very quickly.
4 Drive-in movie theatres were popular.
5 The tweezers were made for the cosmetic industry.

A holiday dance for students

Dal borrowed money from a friend to set up a dance party for students coming home for their holidays.

Computer dating

Dal organised a dance party in 1967 that matched people together using a computer.

Making a movie

Another idea Dal had was to make a movie. He spent two years working on the movie.

Drive-in disco

In the 1960s, it was popular to go to drive-in movie theatres in the USA. Dal had the idea to change these drive-in theatres into drive-in discos.

Tweezerman

Dal started this business with $500 in 1980. He bought industrial tweezers and sold them as cosmetic tweezers.

4 Only one of these businesses was successful. Discuss with a partner which one you think it was.

Listening

5 ◀))) **8.1** Listen to Dal LaMagna's businesses being described. Tick (✓) the box to show whether each business was successful or not.

Successful					
Unsuccessful					

6 Listen again and match each business with the reason for its failure.

1 A holiday dance for students
2 Computer dating
3 Making a movie
4 Drive-in disco

a People didn't use credit cards and couldn't get online.
b He didn't have the experience and couldn't get the money.
c People couldn't get to the event.
d He didn't close the deal and didn't sign the contract.

Grammar

Past simple	
Use the past simple to talk about completed past actions.	
Positive	
I/He/She/It was You/We/They were	
All other forms of the past simple are the same for all pronouns.	
Regular past verbs end in *-ed.* finished, worked	
Many verbs in English have an irregular past form.	get – got, have – had, do – did
Negative	**Questions**
Use *didn't* + infinitive (without *to*).	Use *did* + infinitive (without *to*)
I/He/She/It/We/You/They didn't sell many tickets.	Did you sell many tickets?

>>>GRAMMAR REFERENCE PAGE 109

More practice

7 Complete the sentences using the correct negative form of the verbs in brackets.

1 I .... (do) the research needed.
2 He .... (remember) to sign the contract.
3 There .... (be) a market for the product because people .... (have) the technology.
4 He .... (plan) well because he spent all of his profits.
5 The companies .... (be) successful and closed.
6 People .... (use) credit cards then, so it .... (work).

8 Change the sentences from negative to positive.

1 The computer system didn't work effectively.
2 The company didn't make an effective long-term plan.
3 I didn't leave early enough to get my plane.
4 I didn't arrive on time for the meeting.
5 She wasn't able to contact the customer.
6 He didn't read the instruction manual carefully.

Vocabulary

9 Complete the sentences with words and phrases from the box in the correct form.

> fail   failure   fault   get it right   make a mistake   not work
> success   weakness

1 It was a good idea, but the one .... was that it was too expensive.
2 I .... by not planning well enough.
3 The product was a .... because there was too much competition.
4 The concept .... in Germany, but it was a success in America.
5 It took many attempts to .... , but eventually the idea was a success.
6 The company .... People were just not interested in the product.
7 It took a lot of investment to make the product a .... , but now it is one of the company's top products.
8 Lots of people made mistakes, but no one would say it was their ....

More practice

Speaking

10 Think about yourself, your company or another company you know well. Look at the areas for making possible mistakes in the box. Can you think of something you or the company did wrong for each?

> deadline   giving directions   idea   investment   plan   price   product

11 Use your ideas and words from **10** to tell a partner what happened.

I bought shares in Nokia. The investment failed and I lost money.
Our company asked for too much money for X and it failed.

Ingvar Kamprad

Roman Abramovich

Amancio Ortega

Sara Blakely

Warren Buffett

Start up

1 Look at the pictures and tell a partner what you know about each person.

2 Match each person with the business they helped set up.

1 Ingvar Kamprad	**a** Zara
The founder of an international furniture retailer, worth about $31 billion today. He started selling matches.	
2 Roman Abramovich	**b** Sibneft
The Russian owner of Chelsea FC. He made his fortune in oil and is worth about $23 billion. He started out selling plastic ducks.	
3 Amancio Ortega	**c** IKEA
The Spanish owner of a worldwide clothes retailer. Today he is worth about $20 billion, but his first job was as a shop assistant.	
4 Warren Buffett	**d** Spanx
The American investment banker is worth about $37 billion today. He started out selling chewing gum, Coca-Cola and magazines door-to-door.	
5 Sara Blakely	**e** Berkshire Hathaway
In 2012, she was the youngest self-made female billionaire on the Forbes rich list at $1 billion. She made money as a teenager when people paid to come into a Hallowe'en haunted house she made.	

3))) **8.2** Listen and check your answers.

4 Which successful business people do you admire? Tell your partner about them.

Listening ⑤ Look at the seven factors affecting success. Discuss with a partner which two you think are least important.

1 Being honest is the best policy. People who tell lies soon get into trouble.

5 You have to be passionate about what you do – even if that is just about making money.

2 Being disciplined is important for success. It's important to get things done even when you don't want to do them.

6 Nearly all successful business people are also lucky people. It's about being in the right place at the right time.

3 You need to be respectful and appreciative of others. Nobody is a success on their own.

7 Highly educated people from top universities are nearly always successful.

4 Hard-working people aren't always successful, but all successful people are hard-working.

⑥ •))) 8.3 Temi has just read a book on success in business. Listen to her discussing it with a colleague over lunch. Which two factors in ⑤ are not important in being successful?

> honesty   discipline   being respectful and appreciative
> being hard-working   passion   luck   education

⑦ Listen again. Which reasons does Karl give for not agreeing with the book?

1 No one will say they're rich because they're lucky.
2 Many dishonest people are successful.
3 He's well educated and has a job.

Vocabulary ⑧ Complete the sentences with the highlighted words in ⑤.

1 He's very .... Even when he doesn't want to do a task, he makes sure he works to the best of his ability and finishes it on time.
2 She's very .... of other people's opinions. Even when she disagrees strongly, she's polite about it.
3 She's so .... about the project. You can see it really excites her.
4 Many people think a lot of successful business people tell lies, but being .... is thought to be an important factor in being successful.
5 It was a really bad mistake. He was .... not to lose his job.
6 He's very .... and spends ten hours a day in the office. He's almost never off his Blackberry.
7 It's important to be .... , but sometimes in business common sense is more important.
8 I wish my boss was more .... of all my hard work. He doesn't seem to care how many hours I work.

More practice

Speaking ⑨ Write down three things in your life you think were successes.

⑩ Match vocabulary from ⑧ with each of your successes.

⑪ Tell a partner about your successes from ⑨ and ⑩ and the reasons for them. Ask questions to find out more.

75

Start up

1 Work with a partner. Ask and answer the questions.

1 How many meetings do you have in a week?
2 What meeting do you have the most often?
3 What's the focus of the meetings you have to attend?

2 Why do companies have so many meetings? Think of different reasons for having meetings.

Reading

3 Read the text and match the mistake people made with a piece of advice.

Successful meetings

1 Firstly, make sure the meeting is necessary and has a clear goal. It's not a good idea to waste people's time.

2 Make sure everyone is prepared by sending out an agenda and the venue in plenty of time. The meeting will be much more effective.

3 A meeting isn't a social event. Invite only the participants you really need and try to have a chair who keeps to the time allowed.

4 For a series of meetings, make sure the minutes are sent to everyone to read before the next meeting, with clear action points set for people to do by a given deadline.

a *No one knew where it was or what it was about.*

c *At least half the people didn't need to be there.*

b *I didn't really know why we had the meeting this morning.*

d *No one did any work between one meeting and the next.*

4 When people don't do one of the things in the text, how do you feel? Tell a partner.

Vocabulary

5 Complete the sentences with highlighted words or phrases from the text in **4**.

1 I'm happy to be a .... in a meeting, but I don't like to lead a meeting.
2 Our secretary usually takes the .... , so we know what was decided.
3 I hate meetings with no clear .... What's the point of meeting when we don't know what we want to achieve?
4 .... must be completed before the next meeting.
5 When people miss a .... , it can make everyone late.
6 The .... for our meeting was horrible. Eight hours in a room with no windows!
7 The .... had no control of the meeting. Everyone was talking at the same time.
8 No one was prepared because someone forgot to send out an .... before the meeting.

More practice

Listening

6))) **8.4** Listen to the start of a meeting and complete the minutes.

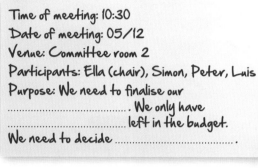

Time of meeting: 10:30
Date of meeting: 05/12
Venue: Committee room 2
Participants: Ella (chair), Simon, Peter, Luis
Purpose: We need to finalise our
.... We only have
.... left in the budget.
We need to decide ....

7))) **8.5** Listen to another part of the meeting. Complete the action points.

Action point: Luis needs to look for the cost of ....
Deadline: ....

8 Listen again and complete the phrases.

1 .... try to decide on some actual destinations?
2 .... agreeing on two main strategies first?
3 .... the main options are …
4 I .... , because in a country so big …
5 I .... , but most of the important business centres are on the coast.
6 I .... that, even north to south is far.

Action point: Peter needs to email ....
Deadline: Next meeting

9 Complete the phrases for suggesting, giving opinions and agreeing with words from the box.

about	agree	but	doubt	know	sure	that	think	we / I

Suggesting	Giving opinions	Agreeing	Disagreeing
Shall .... ?	I	I	I see what you mean, ...
How .... ?	I'm not	Definitely, without	I don't .... about ....

10 Listen to the meeting again and check your answers.

Speaking

11 Look at the opinions. Work with a partner to think of: a reason to agree, a reason to disagree, and a suggestion you could make.

1 I think we should work a four-day week.
2 I think we should be able to retire at 55.
3 I think university should be compulsory.

12 Work with another group. Take turns to agree, disagree or make a suggestion.

Scenario: A dysfunctional team

1 ◊)) **8.6** Wildings is an international food manufacturer in France. Pierre has asked Alex and Zafira, two of the company's product managers, to create a team of four people from their two teams to help develop and launch a new product. Listen to their discussion and make a note of the job titles.

	George	Benoît	Amy	Emilie
Job title				

2 Listen again and make a note of the reason why each person has been recommended.

	George	Benoît	Amy	Emilie
Reason				

3 Zafira and Alex need to decide who will lead the group. Discuss with a partner who you think they will choose and why.

	George	Benoît	Amy	Emilie
Reason				

4 ◢)) **8.7** Listen to the first meeting. Tick (✓) the correct option in each case.

Benoît	wrote an agenda	☐	didn't write an agenda	☐
George	is on time	☐	is late	☐
Emilie	can stay all day	☐	can't stay all day	☐
Amy	is very busy	☐	isn't very busy	☐

5 Listen again. Match the people with the action points.

1	George	a	Bring competitor designs
2	Benoît	b	Bring a financial spreadsheet
3	Amy	c	Access everyone's calendars
4	Emilie	d	Write an agenda

6 ◢)) **8.8** Listen to their second meeting and complete Benoît's notes.

George didn't like the .... designs.
Must remember to send .... earlier.
Amy .... the spreadsheet.
Emilie .... future meetings.

7 Think back to your choice in **3**. Did you choose Benoît? Based on the meetings, what skills doesn't he have to lead a team?

8 Work in groups of four. Students A and B, see below. Student C, look at page 97. Student D, look at page 101. Have a meeting and discuss how to improve things.

Student A - Amy

You don't think that Benoît ran the meetings well. He isn't very disciplined – give at least two examples of mistakes he made.

Suggest ways of improving the meeting

Student B - George

You agree with Amy about the meetings.

You think Benoît didn't allow you to be passionate and creative.

Suggest that you are given responsibility for design.

Start up

1 Look at the different rules and decide how true they are for your company.

1 arrive and leave at a fixed time
2 share an office/desk/computer
3 make personal phone calls
4 take tea/coffee/lunch breaks when you want to
5 look up things on the internet not for work
6 send personal emails
7 wear a suit and tie/smart clothes to work

2 Compare your answers with a partner. Are there any other rules for your company?

Listening

3 It's Orlando Volpone's first day at 121 Insurance. His new boss is taking him round the office. Before you listen, try to complete the company rules with the words in the box.

any time	earrings	four	shirt	suit	ten

121 INSURANCE

■ **Core working hours**
All staff must be in the building between ....[1] and ....[2].

■ **The dress code for men**
We don't expect male employees to wear a ....[3], but they need to wear a ....[4] and tie to work – no ....[5].

■ **Lunch breaks**
Staff can take a one-hour lunch break. You can take the lunch break ....[6].

4))) **9.1** Listen and check your answers.

5 Complete the sentences with *can, can't, has to, have to, don't have to* or *doesn't have to*. Listen again and check.

1 Orlando .... wear a suit to work.
2 Orlando .... start work at eight if he wants to.
3 Staff .... use a swipe card to enter and leave the building.
4 Male staff at 121 Insurance .... wear anything they want.
5 Orlando .... take tea or coffee breaks when he wants to.
6 He .... tell his boss when he goes for lunch.
7 Smoking isn't allowed, but you .... smoke outside the building.

Grammar

> **Modal verbs – *can* and *have to***
>
> Use *can* and *can't* to say something is or isn't possible or allowed.
>
> Staff can't smoke in the building, but you can smoke on the terrace outside.
>
> Use *have/has to* and *don't/doesn't have to* to say that something is or isn't necessary.
>
> You don't have to wear a suit to work, but you have to wear a smart shirt and tie.

>>>GRAMMAR REFERENCE PAGE 109

6 Complete the sentences with the correct forms of *can/can't* and *have to/don't have to*. Sometimes there is more than one possible answer.

1 You .... smoke in here. It's against company regulations!
2 He .... come to lunch with us if he doesn't want to.
3 I .... arrive early tomorrow. I've got a meeting at 8.30.
4 All visitors to the company .... sign the visitors' book when they enter the building.
5 It's six o' clock. You .... go home now.
6 She .... tell her boss if she wants to leave early.

More practice

Speaking

7 Work with a partner. Ask and answer the questions.

1 What dress code rules are there in your company?
2 What hours do you have to work?
3 What are the rules about breaks?
4 Can you smoke at work?
5 Can you use your phone and computer for personal calls and emails?

Start up

1 What's your job title in your own language? How do you say it in English? Complete the sentences and tell your partner.

1 I work (in an office/factory/school/at home, etc.) in (city/town).
2 My job is to (organise/sell/buy/look after/repair/make, etc.).
3 I'm responsible for …

Reading

2 Look at the titles of the two texts below about different jobs. Translate the job titles into your language and discuss what you know about each job with a partner.

3 Read the texts. Answer the questions.

1 Who: has to work shifts?
    sometimes has to work at night?
2 What does the defence lawyer do in the evening?
3 What can happen to the defence lawyer at night?
4 What can't you do if you work in the control room of a nuclear power plant?
5 What does the nuclear reactor operator have to do in an emergency?

4 Read the texts again. <u>Underline</u> examples of language that show something:

1 is/isn't possible 2 is/isn't allowed 3 is/isn't necessary.

The criminal defence lawyer

(Salary: £ 70,000 pa as a partner in the firm)

Mahua Pandit-Taylor, 36, is a criminal defence lawyer. She works in the firm's offices in the city centre, but usually spends two days a week in court. Twice a month, she's on night duty at the local police station. She doesn't have to sleep there, but the police can call on her from 5.00 p.m. to 8.30 a.m. Her job is to advise people who the police have arrested for crimes and to represent them in court. She often has to work very long hours. She starts at 7.00 a.m. and works until 5.00 p.m., when she goes home to put her children to bed. She often has to go back to the office in the evening and she works until midnight.

The nuclear reactor operator

(Salary: €47,613 to €57,029)

Quentin Mauriac, 51, works at the Saint Barthélemy nuclear power plant in the Midi Pyrenees region in France. He's a nuclear reactor operator and manages a team of 120 staff. It's his team's job to control and monitor the nuclear reactor 24 hours a day, seven days a week. During the week, he works shifts and his hours are either 8.00 a.m. to 2.00 p.m., 2.00 p.m. to 10.00 p.m. or 10.00 p.m. to 8.00 a.m. The staff on duty in the control room aren't allowed to read during their shift and they aren't allowed to leave the control room empty.
If there are sudden changes in the reactor, they have to know what to do and they have to act quickly. In an emergency, Quentin is responsible for operating the red button which makes the reactor shut down immediately.

Listening

5 9.2 **Listen to an interview with Gabriel and choose the correct option in each statement.**

1 He manages *279 / 289* staff.
2 He starts work at *6.00 a.m. / 7.00 a.m.*
3 Sometimes there are *20 / 80* boxes waiting to go on the shelves.

6 **Listen again and complete the questions.**

1 What days of the week .... you .... work?
2 .... you choose the hours you work?
3 .... you .... work nights?
4 .... you open later?

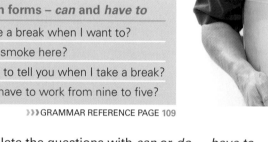

Grammar

Question forms – *can* and *have to*
Can I take a break when I want to?
Can they smoke here?
Do I have to tell you when I take a break?
Does he have to work from nine to five?

››› GRAMMAR REFERENCE PAGE 109

7 **Complete the questions with *can* or *do ... have to.***

More practice

work till six *Do you have to work until six?*

1 .... take a two-hour lunch break
2 .... leave early on Fridays
3 .... wear a uniform
4 .... use the computers for personal email
5 .... work on Saturdays

Say it right

8 **Look at the phrases and answer 1–3.**

I can smoke in my office. *Can you park at work?* *Yes, I can.* *No, I can't.*

1 Practise saying the sentences with a partner.
2 What differences do you notice in how *can* and *can't* are pronounced?
3 9.3 Listen and check.

Speaking

9 **Interview some other students about their job. Write at least three questions. Use *can* and *have to* in some of the questions, but not all of them. Use the ideas in the box to help you. Interview two or three students in the class.**

colleagues emergencies food and drink holidays problems responsibilities transport

Start up

1 **Discuss the questions with a partner.**

1 Who do you send emails to in English?

2 How many emails in English do you send

   a a week?   **b** a month?

3 What are the emails usually about?

Reading

2 **Read the two emails and answer the questions.**

1 Who already works at Communicon?

   a Colin   **b** Sally   **c** Fiona

2 Which two people are friends?

   a Colin and Fiona   **b** Sally and Fiona   **c** Sally and Colin

3 Which email is formal and which is informal?

4 Read the advert and make a list of the tasks in the job and the skills the person needs.

A

To: colin.campbell@gmail.com
From: f.russell@communicon.co.uk
Subject: Your application

Dear Mr Campbell,
We are delighted to be able to offer you the position of Customer Service Representative. Please find attached a formal letter of engagement. If you would like to accept the position, could you print it and send a signed copy back to me?
The position would start on Monday 15th, but before this I would like to ask you to come for another quick meeting on the 7th. I would be grateful if you could confirm that these dates are suitable.
I look forward to seeing you again.
Yours sincerely
Fiona Russell
Human Resources Assistant

B

To: s.alesco@communicon.co.uk
From: colin.campbell@gmail.com
Subject: Job

Hi Sally,
I got the job as Customer Service representative! I've attached the job advert. They want me to start in a fortnight. I just wanted to ask you some information about the company (unofficial information!). Can you tell me about the clothes, hours, work, etc.?
Really excited about the job!
It'll be great to see you again!
All the best
Colin

COMUNICOM

Customer Service Representative

A position is available for the right candidate to work in our busy customer service team. Your role will involve answering customer enquiries on the phone and answering letters of complaint. You will also help maintain our customer service records. You will need to be able to work well on your own but to also have excellent teamwork skills. A polite and friendly telephone manner is essential.

SALARY ON APPLICATION

Please send your CV to f.russell@communicom.co.uk

Vocabulary

3 Look at these beginnings and endings. Place them on the line from most formal to most informal.

| Dear Colin | Dear Mr Campbell | Dear Sir | Hi Colin |

| All the best | Best wishes/Best regards | Cheers |

| Yours faithfully | Yours sincerely |

formal---informal

More practice

4 Find the formal equivalents of the informal expressions in the emails in this lesson.

Informal	Formal
I attach …	
Can you …	
It will be great to see you again.	

Writing

5 Look at the expressions and decide whether you think they would be used in Colin's reply to Fiona Russell (C) or Sally's reply to Colin (S).

1 I'm delighted to …
2 Excellent news!
3 Please find attached a scan of …
4 You'll have to …
5 The start date would be fine and I can make the meeting on …
6 See you soon.
7 I look forward to …
8 Yours faithfully

6 Use the phrases in **5** to write Colin and Sally's replies.

Reading

7 Complete the dos and don'ts of email etiquette with the words in the box.

> abbreviations   CAPITAL LETTERS   emoticons 😊   high priority
> language   reply   short   subject line

Don't

✗ write in ....[1] – it's like shouting at someone.
✗ use ....[2] too often or people will not believe you and ignore it.
✗ use ....[3] unless you know people will understand them.
✗ use ....[4] – they can look unprofessional.

Do

✓ include a meaningful ....[5] , as people are more likely to read it.
✓ make emails as ....[6] as possible so that people read them.
✓ hit ....[7] and not 'new mail' or people will waste time trying to find old messages.
✓ check the ....[8] especially spelling, grammar and punctuation.

8 The email below should be formal, but it is too informal. Correct the mistakes to make it more formal.

To: e.lourdes@gmail.com
From: k.m.pyper@hotmail.co.uk
Subject:
Hi Emma,
I've attached my CV. Can you let me know when the interviews are? It'll be great to meet you.
All the best
Kamila

Scenario: Problems at reception

1 🔊 **9.4** Durmin is an international logistics company based in Austria. You're going to hear four people who work at the reception desk talking. Write their hours of work.

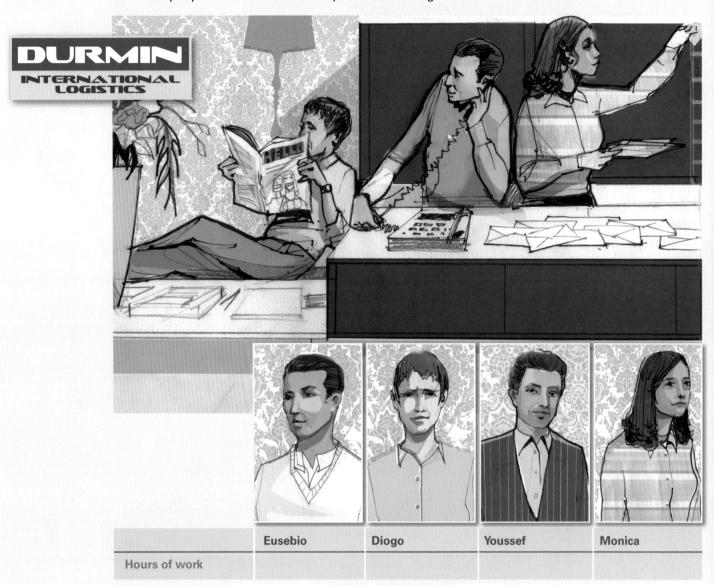

	Eusebio	Diogo	Youssef	Monica
Hours of work				

2 Listen again and write the information about each person.

	Eusebio	Diogo	Youssef	Monica
Likes about the job				
Dislikes about the job				

3 🔊 **9.5** Listen to four short incidents at reception. Match the incidents with the problems.

Incident 1	a	not focused on the job
Incident 2	b	laziness
Incident 3	c	poor English
Incident 4	d	no one at the desk

4 Youssef receives three emails about reception. What are the problems?

To: y.elquatami@durmin.com
From: hr@durmin.com
Subject: Missed English classes

Dear Mr Elquatami,
I'm writing to you regarding your staff's lack of attendance at the English classes provided. These classes cost a lot of money and are provided for both the benefit of the individual and the company. We really need to make sure all our staff's English is of a good standard. Could you explain your staff's absence, please?
Kind regards
Kamala

To: y.elquatami@durmin.com
From: hr@durmin.com
Subject: Staff performance

Dear Youssef,
We have received a number of complaints recently about the appearance of staff on reception. One customer said that they were dressed more for the beach than work. He also felt that they were quite rude. Could you please speak to your staff about this issue?
Regards
Kara

To: y.elquatami@durmin.com
From: hr@durmin.com
Subject: Discipline

Dear Youssef,
The problems at reception are really getting out of control. Today we received a complaint that two of your staff were shouting and screaming at each other. They said it was like watching a soap opera on TV. This really is unacceptable and needs to be dealt with.
Regards
Kara

5 Discuss with a partner what action you think Youssef should take.

6 9.6 Youssef is called to a meeting by his boss. What does his boss think is wrong and what does he want Youssef to do about it?

7 Work with a partner to suggest an action plan for Youssef to solve the problem.

8 Write an email to Eusebio, Monica and Diogo. In the email, explain:

- company dress code
- when breaks can be taken
- the hours they are expected to work
- the responsibilities they have as a team.

10 A helping hand
Making decisions
will for spontaneous decisions and promises

Start up

1 Work with a partner and discuss what is happening in each of the pictures.

2 List five decisions you made this week from the easiest to the hardest. Tell a partner the reasons for the order.

Reading

3 Discuss with a partner what you think the benefits of mentoring are.

4 Read the text. Are your ideas from **3** mentioned?

> **?**
>
> A **mentor** is a person with a lot of experience who helps someone with less experience for a period of time.

Mentors

Over 70% of the 500 largest companies in the USA have a mentoring programme.

However, the old model of 'your boss is your mentor' is no longer the normal model, with people seeking help from a wider range of contacts. You don't have to be that old or experienced to pass on knowledge or even very high up the hierarchy.

Mentoring is becoming common in the business world, but is it worth the time and effort? A study by Gartner, an American research firm, found that:

- 25% of employees on a mentoring programme had a promotion, but only 5% of workers not taking part had a promotion

- mentors were promoted six times more often than those not in a mentoring programme

- mentees were promoted five times more often than those not in a mentoring programme.

Some people fear that sharing their experience with their younger colleagues will put their own jobs at risk. They want your job, don't they? Well, they might want your job, but mentoring or not mentoring them isn't going to change that.

Making a difference to the lives of others can help make people happier. Some of the happiest people, no matter what their normal job is, are helping others through life's difficulties.

5 Read the text again. Are the sentences true or false?

1 Most large US companies have a mentoring programme.
2 It's better to be much older when giving advice.
3 Mentoring is helpful for the person being mentored and the mentor.
4 Mentors are more likely to get promoted.
5 Mentors sometimes worry that their mentee might want their job.
6 Mentoring is stressful and won't make you happy.

Listening

6 •))) **10.1** Listen to Lia talking to her mentor, José. What does Lia decide to do in each situation?

1 Lia's colleague keeps talking loudly on the phone.
   a ask José to speak to him ☐
   b wear headphones and listen to music ☐
2 Lia's finding a computer program difficult
   a practise at home ☐
   b book a training course ☐
3 Lia's struggling to manage her time.
   a ask for extra support ☐
   b go on a time management course ☐

7 Listen again and complete the sentences.

1 That's a good idea. I .... do that.
2 I .... have time. I .... just practise at home.
3 I think I .... book myself a place.

Grammar

> **will for spontaneous decisions and promises**
>
> Use *will* for an instant decision and agreeing to do something at the moment of speaking.
>
> I'll have the pizza, please.
>
> I won't have time to walk. I'll take the train.
>
> We also use it for making offers.
>
> A: A new client is arriving this afternoon.
> B: I'll show him round. Then I'll take him to his hotel.

⟫⟫GRAMMAR REFERENCE PAGE 109

8 Match the question or comments with the decisions.

1	What would you like?	a	I'll come as well.
2	We're going out for a drink tonight.	b	I'll shut it down.
3	You've left your computer on again.	c	I'll have a black coffee, please.
4	I've got too much work on.	d	I'll call her. What's it about?
5	I haven't got time to phone Ruby.	e	I'll help you. I've got some spare time.

More practice

9 Write your decision for each of the situations.

1 It's noisy outside and you are the nearest person to the window.
   I'll close the window.
2 You want the salad, not vegetables.
   ....
3 Your boss wants someone to finish the report. You don't have time today but you will tomorrow.
   ....
4 You meet a visitor at reception with a large bag.
   ....

Speaking

10 You have one minute to make these decisions. Tell your partner what you will do.

1 You have a lot of work to do, but there is a programme you want to watch on TV.
   I'll watch television and work at the same time.
2 You can only promote one person in your department (not yourself).
3 You can have any desk in the office.
4 You can have any car you want.
5 You can have any job in the company you want.

Start up

1 Look at the pictures and discuss the questions with a partner.

1 What do you think is happening in the pictures?
2 Does your company send employees on teambuilding events?
3 What type of person do you think would be successful in each event?
4 Which event would you most like to do and why?

Reading

2 You're going to read a text on creating a team. What types of people do you need for a good team?

3 Read the text and match headings 1–3 with sections A–C.

1 People roles   2 Intellectual roles   3 Action roles

Why do some teams work better than others? Meredith Belbin suggested that it's the different personalities and skills that make a team succeed or fail. So what different types of people does an effective team need?

A ....
This is the group that likes to do things.
The shaper is energetic and determined to get things going.
The implementer is reliable and efficient and turns ideas into practical actions.
The completer-finisher looks for mistakes and errors. They're perfectionists and punctual.

B ....
This is the group with the best people skills.
The co-ordinator brings everything together and delegates well. They're confident and mature.
The team worker is cooperative, listens to everyone and avoids conflict.
The resource investigator has lots of contacts and is a natural networker.
They are enthusiastic and communicative, but not good at finishing work.

C ....
These are the ideas people.
The plant is creative, comes up with the original ideas and solves difficult problems.
The monitor/evaluator is strategic and good at judging situations. They see and evaluate all options.
The specialist has good knowledge on a subject. They're dedicated and self-starting.

4 Match the people with different roles in the text.

1 I don't have a lot of new ideas, but I know how to make ideas work in real life.

2 I worry a lot and have to check everything very carefully.

3 I'm always calming everyone down and stopping fights.

4 I always know who to contact to help me with a problem.

5 People often go with the first idea that comes into their head. I'm good at looking at all the choices.

6 I love the start of a project, but get bored with the reality of the work.

Vocabulary

5 Choose from the pair of words to complete the sentences.

1 She's very *reliable / energetic* – she always does the work she's asked very well and on time.

4 He's a *strategic / creative* thinker. He's good at planning and organising projects.

More practice

2 He's very *confident / punctual* and never misses a deadline.

5 She's an *efficient / determined* person. She never gives up.

3 It's important to be *cooperative / reliable* in my job. I have to work with some difficult people.

6 They're such a *dedicated / enthusiastic* team. They're always so positive.

6 Choose words not used to complete the sentences above that best describe you. Write a sentence using each word.

Speaking

7 Tell a partner which one(s) from the text you think are most like you and why.

8 Look at the teams. What strengths and weaknesses would each team have?

Team A	Team B
Jan a plant and team worker	Simone a team worker
Jude a monitor/evaluator	Pilar a completer-finisher
Andy an implementer	Roberto a specialist and resource investigator

Start up ① Look at the pictures. What do you think each person is suggesting?

Listening ② ◀)) **10.2** Listen to the conversations.
Match the suggestions a–c with the people 1–3.

1 Franck   **2** Penny   **3** Victor

③ Listen again and complete the sentences.

Franck: It's a lovely day, isn't it?
Anya: It's wonderful. What ....¹ do?
Franck: ....² go to the beach?
Greg: OK, would you ....³?

Sally: Just look at those clouds. I'm not going
out in that.
Penny: Come on. ....⁴ take a taxi.
Sally: ....⁵, but you're paying.

Victor: We haven't got any food in the house.
Anka: Really? ....⁶ get a takeaway.
Victor: Let's eat out.
Anka: That's a ....⁷. I ....⁸ pay.

a

b

c

Functional language

Asking for and making suggestions

We use *shall* to ask for and make suggestions.

Shall we go out for dinner tonight?

What shall we do for lunch?

Other expressions to make suggestions include:

We/You can/could …

Why don't we/you …

Let's …

Offering help

Would you like me to…

Shall I…

Can I…

We also use *will* to make offers.

I'll do it.

Responding positively and negatively to suggestions and offers

Positively – Yes, that's a good idea. / Yes, I agree. / Excellent idea!

Negatively – No, I don't think so. / No, I'm afraid I … / Sorry, but I'm not sure …

4 Rearrange the words to make or ask for suggestions.

1 swimming go shall we ?
2 a drink let's have .
3 don't we walk why ?
4 shall we what do ?
5 could we visit castle the .

5 Work with a partner. Make suggestions and offers using the prompts.

1 go to the cinema   drive
Shall we go to the cinema?   *OK, shall I drive?*
2 have a coffee   make it
3 get something to eat   pay
4 meet again next week   come to my house

Reading

6 Read the emails and answer the questions.

1 What does Keiko want Rosa to organise?
2 Who does Rosa want at the meeting?
3 Does Keiko agree with Rosa's suggestion?

Dear Rosa,
I suggest that we meet to discuss these ideas further. It would be a good idea to have lots of people there. Could you find out when people are free and arrange a meeting?

Kind regards
Keiko

Dear Keiko,
That makes sense. I'd like to propose that we involve the whole department. The more opinions we have the better.

Kind regards
Rosa

Dear Rosa,
That sounds really interesting, but it's not what we are looking for. We need to be focused. I suggest that we keep the meeting small.

Kind regards
Keiko

7 Complete the phrases for making and responding to formal suggestions.

1 I .... that we …
2 It would be a .... to …
3 That makes ....
4 I'd like to .... that we …
5 That sounds really ....
6 It's not really what we're .... for.

Listening

8 10.3 Listen to a phone call extract discussing alternative suggestions to those in **6**. Make a note of the alternative suggestions.

1 Setting up ....
2 Starting an ....
3 Setting up a ....

Writing

9 Write a formal email to respond to the suggestions in the phone call with further suggestions of how to involve everyone.

1 Abdulrahman is a team leader in an insurance firm. He is worried about how the team are working together. Read his email to his boss Maxim and match each team member with a strength and a weakness.

		Strengths	Weaknesses
1	Sergio	confident	not punctual
2	Tosh	reliable	not communicative
3	Hang	energetic	not cooperative
4	Hanan	dedicated	not enthusiastic
5	Ryoko	creative	not efficient

Hi Maxim,
I'm having some problems with my team at the moment. Individually they all have strengths, but they're not working very well together.

Sergio always does everything you ask, but he just never tells anyone what he's doing. People get nervous about progress just because he doesn't talk to anyone about his projects. Tosh has a great belief in himself and his abilities, which is great – you can give him work and really believe he will do it. The problem is it's never on time. Hang has so many original and different ideas, but she just works so slowly. Hanan is the opposite – she's always busy doing something and fills the room with life. She just won't work with other people. Ryoko puts in so much time and effort, but she just appears so bored by everything.

I really feel I need some help with this team. Have you got time for a meeting to discuss what I could do?

Best wishes
Abdulrahman

2)) **10.4** Listen to the first part of a meeting between Abdulrahman and Maxim. Tick (✓) the suggestions Maxim makes.

1 Organise a team meeting
2 Email everyone for suggestions
3 Organise a motivational speaker
4 Organise an awayday

3 Discuss with a partner which option you would prefer if you were having problems in a team at work.

4 Abdulrahman decides to research the options for awaydays. Work in groups of three. Read the texts on page 95, paying attention to the underlined information. Complete the notes that follow.

Forest challenge

Take part in an active outdoor team event. Sessions last for half a day or a full day and are for groups of 6 to 25 people. This is a competitive team event involving teamwork, leadership, problem-solving and decision-making skills.

Teams navigate their way to a number of problem-solving challenge sites in a forest, to arrive by a specified time.

Teams need to focus on priorities. At each challenge site, teams undertake a different team challenge. Problem-solving challenges use different qualities and skills from within the team.

This is an ideal event for an awayday for an active team that seeks a real challenge in the great outdoors – a challenge that requires teamwork and commitment and brings a great sense of achievement.

Creative challenge

Take part in an outdoor high-tech team-building activity. Sessions last two to three hours and are for 5 to 20 people. The Creative Challenge is a fun-filled and challenging team game that lets your participants get to know each other better, think creatively and work as a team.

Teams of 2-3 members compete against each other in solving problems in a game area of your choosing. This could be a city centre, a village or the gardens and grounds of a hotel or conference centre. Each team is sent missions to their mobile phone.

The technology we use is great fun and gives instant feedback each time they respond to a question or mission. And all responses on the mobile phones are stored instantly and we let everyone know which team is currently in the lead.

Bushcraft challenge

Take part in a two-day outdoor team-building event for 5 to 25 people. Your aircraft crashed in the mountains! You and your companions need to live in the wild until help arrives.

Teams initially decide on priorities and then set out to find essential equipment in the area. Teams then make emergency shelters and light fires. You also catch, prepare and eat your own food.

These activities help build an understanding of the natural world. They also create an incredible team spirit as you work together overcoming real challenges. This is a unique and genuinely memorable team-building event. You'll come away from your Bushcraft Challenge event feeling tired but with an experience that your team will talk about for weeks and months to come!

---

1 Might be too ....
The group might fight.

2 Good for the team to appreciate each other's ....

3 Will everyone have the .... needed?

---

1 Will it be good for people who aren't .... ?

2 Having too small .... might cause problems: I want one team.

3 Do I want one team to be .... and the other to lose?

---

1 We will have to stay ....
Will this make people happy?

2 Will people eat .... they caught?

3 Could make the team really ....

---

5 Discuss with a partner which event would best suit Abdulrahman's team. Think about people's strengths and weaknesses and give reasons why.

Pairwork

Ask your partner questions to help you complete the profiles with the correct words in the box. Answer your partner's questions.

Is his name Peter? No, it isn't.   Is he Austrian?   Yes, he is.

British	Danish	Daphne	doctor	Frühoff	German	Goodman
Lars	lawyer	Olssen	teacher	Ursula		

1
First name ....
Surname ....
Nationality ....
Job ....

2
First name ....
Surname ....
Nationality ....
Job ....

3
First name ....
Surname ....
Nationality ....
Job ....

4
First name Leandro
Surname Brito
Nationality Portuguese
Job accounts manager

5
First name Lili
Surname Wong
Nationality Chinese
Job shop assistant

6
First name Dieter
Surname Urbach
Nationality German
Job office worker

Unit 1 page 9

Student A

1 Greet students B and C.
2 Listen to student B.
3 You forgot your business cards, so take turns to ask for each other's email addresses and phone numbers.

Your phone number – 00 44 1284 356 888
Email address – h.g.mattar@yahoo.com

Unit 3 page 27

Student A

1 Nina is Nick's mother. It's her 70th birthday.
2 Federico is Nick's colleague and Nick doesn't like him.
3 Nick knows that Federico isn't busy. He goes salsa dancing with his girlfriend on Tuesdays.

Unit 4 page 33

Student A

Situation 1. You would like to book a room for three nights. You want to arrive on the 18th and check out on the 21st. You want to know – is the internet free in the rooms and is the gym 24 hours?

Situation 2. You work in the Mirador hotel. The hotel is not near the train station but it is near the airport. It has room service from 6.00 a.m. until midnight.

Unit 6 page 59

Student A

Your friend is going to London at the same time as you. Ask questions to find out the following and arrange a time and day to meet.

My travel information		My friend's travel information	
Flying out:	7.00 p.m. 13th April	**Flying out:**	....
Arriving:	10.00 p.m. 13th April	**Arriving:**	....
Staying at:	Travelodge	**Staying at:**	....
Plans:	14th April shopping on Oxford Street;	**Plans:**	....
	15th April 11.00 – 12.00 p.m. visiting the	**Leaving:**	....
	Tower of London		
Leaving:	17th April 7.00 a.m.		

Unit 8 page 79

Student C

Benoît: You know the team aren't happy. You agree you made mistakes, but you think people should be more respectful and appreciate your position. Other people didn't do what they had to do. Point out other people's mistakes. Suggest that everyone needs to take responsibility.

Answer your partner's questions. Ask your partner questions to help you complete the profiles with the correct words in the box.

Is his name Peter? No, it isn't.   Is he Austrian?   Yes, he is.

| accounts manager | Brito | Chinese | Dieter | German | Leandro | Lili |
| office worker | Portuguese | | shop assistant | Urbach | Wong | |

1
First name	Daphne
Surname	Goodman
Nationality	British
Job	lawyer

2
First name	Ursula
Surname	Frühoff
Nationality	German
Job	doctor

3
First name	Lars
Surname	Olssen
Nationality	Danish
Job	teacher

  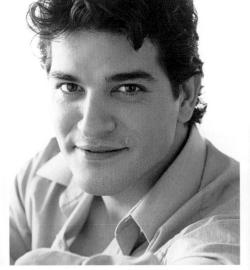

4
First name	....
Surname	....
Nationality	....
Job	....

5
First name	....
Surname	....
Nationality	....
Job	....

6
First name	....
Surname	....
Nationality	....
Job	....

Unit 1 page 9

Student B

1 Greet students A and C.
2 Introduce Student A to Student C.
3 You forgot your business cards, so take turns to ask for each other's email addresses and phone numbers.

Your phone number – 00 52 987 611 190
Email address – p.reina19@gmail.com

Unit 1 page 11, exercise 3

Student B

○ ○ ○

manal.obeid@iqbal.com; j.fernandes@estrella.es; h_wu@gmail.com

Hi Henry, Javier and Manal,
I'm sorry but 9 is not good for me. My flight gets in at 8.45. Can we meet at 10?
My number is 07998 883 421 and the country code is 0049.
See you tomorrow
Agna

○ ○ ○

j.fernandes@estrella.es; schmid.agna@kryptosoft.hu; h_wu@gmail.com

Hi everyone,
10 is fine for me. My number is 07683 330 219 and the country code is 00961.
Best wishes
Manal

Unit 1 page 11, exercise 6

Student B

You are Mr Wu's colleague, Mr Wang.

Mr Wang
COMPUTER PROGRAMMER
Chinese
07889255691
k.wang@yahoo.com

Greet Javier.
Find out:
- His job
- His phone number
- Where he is from
- His email address
Say goodbye.

Unit 3 page 27

Student B

1 Nick doesn't see Nina very often because she lives far away.
2 Federico and Nick do the same job. Sven is going to make one of them manager soon. Sven likes Federico more than Nick.
3 Federico told Sven his mother is ill.

Unit 4 page 33

Student B

Situation 1. You work in the Hathaway hotel. There are only superior suites available when the customer wants to stay. Internet access is $20 per day. The gym is open 24 hours. Confirm if they want to make the reservation.

Situation 2. You would like to book a room for 5 nights. You want to arrive on the 25th and leave on the 1st. You want to know – is the hotel near the train station and does it have 24-hour room service?

WORLD HOTEL

Reviews: A very comfortable and relaxing hotel. The rooms are very quiet and peaceful. It has got an excellent gym and swimming pool. Perfect for relaxing in for business and pleasure.

THE SHERWOOD HOTEL

Reviews: The rooms are nice and clean but quite basic for the price. The award-winning customer service makes this hotel special.

HATHAWAY HOTEL

Reviews: Good value for the price. The standard is high and for a city the price is low! Especially because the internet and breakfast are included in the price.

HOTEL POLO

Reviews: This small family-run hotel is basic but friendly and welcoming. Not for you if you want luxuries!

Unit 5 page 43
Student B

Pepe e Sale

Pepe e Sale is a traditional family restaurant in the centre of town. It is a family-run business. The 60-year-old father and manager is also the owner. One problem working with your family is that they can be difficult to control. I feel like I'm eating my dinner in their family living room. The son, also a waiter in the restaurant, spends most of the evening fighting with his father. They don't pay enough attention to me, not even checking if my food is OK. Unfortunately the staff are not the only thing that makes me feel like I'm eating in their living room. The restaurant may be traditional, but the decoration is out of date. There are too many pictures on the walls, too many things on the table and not enough space. This restaurant is for you if you like waiters who spend too much time talking to each other and not enough time serving you. And it's far too expensive.

Unit 6 page 59
Student B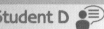

Your friend is going to London at the same time as you. Ask questions to find out the following and arrange a time and day to meet.

My travel information		My friend's travel information	
Flying out:	10.00 a.m. 13th April	Flying out:	....
Arriving:	1.00 p.m. 13th April	Arriving:	....
Staying at:	Travelodge	Staying at:	....
Plans:	14th April taking a train at 11.00 a.m. to see a friend in Oxford; 15th April taking a bus tour 9.00 a.m. to 11.00 a.m.	Plans:	....
		Leaving:	....
Leaving:	16th April 2.00 p.m.		

Unit 1 page 9
Student C

1 Greet Students B and C.
2 Listen to Student B.
3 You forgot your business cards, so take turns to ask for each other's email addresses and phone numbers.

Your phone number – 00 39 2219 887 202
Email address – b.taqi18@hotmail.com

Unit 8 page 79
Student D

Emilie: You are quite happy with the team. Suggest that you help Benoît more with the agenda, minutes and action points. Apologise for not doing the minutes. You think people need a clear role and tasks to do.

Grammar

Unit 1

Present simple *be*

Full form	Short form	Questions	Short answers	
Positive	**Positive**		**Positive**	**Negative**
I am	I'm	Am I hungry?	Yes, I am.	No, I'm not.
You / We / They are	You / We / They're	Are you / we / they hungry?	Yes, you are.	No, you aren't.
He / She / It is	He / She / It's	Is he / she / it hungry?	Yes, he/she is.	No, he/she isn't.
Negative	**Negative**	Where are you from?	Yes, it is.	No, it isn't.
I am not	I'm not	When's dinner?	Yes, we are.	No, we aren't
You / We / They are not	You / We / They aren't	What's the problem?	Yes, they are.	No, they aren't.
He / She / It is not	He / She / It isn't			

When we speak we generally use short forms.
Use full forms:
a) in questions. Example:
Are you a student?
b) in positive short answers.
Example:
Yes, I am.
c) with names or words that end in *s*.
Examples:
James is an engineer.
This is my colleague.

d) in formal writing.
Example:
Dear Mr Smith, We are very pleased to inform you that …
e) for emphasis.
Example:
Susan's colleague: Susan isn't here.
Susan: I am here!

Possessive adjectives, possessive 's

Subject	Possessive adjective
I	my
you	your
he	his
she	her
we	our
you	your
they	their

Use possessive adjectives (*my, your, his,* etc.) before the noun to show possession.
Examples:
my brother, his father, her office, their car

We can also use *'s* after a name or a noun to show possession.
Examples:
This is my friend's sister.
This is Jo's colleague, Tony.

Name	Possessive adjective
Mark	Mark's
Dad	Dad's
Tony	Tony's

Remember!

The *'s* can have two meanings:
a) to show possession.
Example:
John's car

b) the short form of *is*.
Example:
John's from London.

Unit 2

Present simple with *I / You / We / They*

Full form	Questions	Short answer
Positive I / You / We / They work		
Negative I / You / We / They don't work	Do I / you / we / they work on Sundays? Do I / you / we / they start at nine? Do I / you / we / they finish at five?	Yes, I / you / we / they do. No, I / you / we / they don't.
Questions When do you go to work? Where do I go for a meeting? How do they travel to work? Who do you work with? What time do they start work?		

Use the present simple to talk about facts and routines.
Examples:
What do you do?
I work in a record shop. I work six days a week.
I don't work on Sundays.
What do they do?
They work for a TV company. They use computers.
They don't work at weekends.

Note:
These are the full forms of the negative verbs and the negative short answer.
I / You / We / They do not.

Only use these full forms:
a) in formal writing.
b) for emphasis.

have got

Full form	Questions	Short answer
Positive I / You / We / They've got He / She / It's got	Have I / you / we / they got? Has he / she / it got?	Yes, I / you / we / they have. No, I / we / they haven't. Yes, he / she / it has No, he / she / it hasn't.
Negative I / You / We / They haven't got He / She / It hasn't got		

Note:
These are the full forms of the positive and negative verbs and the negative short answer for the third person singular *(he, she, it)*.
He / She / It has got.
He / She / It has not got.
No, he / she / it has not.
Only use these full forms:
a) in formal writing.
b) for emphasis.

Unit 3

Present simple with *He / She / It*

Full form	Questions	Short answers
Positive He / She / It works		
Negative He / She / It doesn't work	Does he / she / it work? Does he / she / it start at nine? Does he / she / it finish at five?	Yes, he / she / it does. No, he / she / it doesn't.
Questions When does he go to work? Where does she need to go for the meeting? How does he travel to work? Who does she work with? What time does it start?		

Use the present simple to talk about facts and routines.
Examples:
Where does she live?
She lives in Hong Kong.
What does he do?
He works in a record shop. He works six days a week. He doesn't work on Sundays.
What does she do?
She works for a TV company. She uses a computer. She doesn't work at weekends.

To make the third person singular:
a) most verbs   + s
Example:
live ▶ lives
b) verbs ending in *-s, -sh, -ch* or *-x*   + es
Example:
kiss ▶ kisses, wish ▶ wishes, teach ▶ teaches, fix ▶ fixes
c) verbs ending in consonant + *y*   *y + ies*
Example:
try ▶ tries, marry ▶ marries
d) verbs ending in vowel + *y*   + s
Example:
say ▶ says, play ▶ plays
e) exceptions:
go ▶ goes, do ▶ does, have ▶ has

Note:
These are the full forms of the negative verbs
and the negative short answer.
He / She / It does not.
Only use these full forms:
a) in formal writing.
b) for emphasis.

like / love / hate / enjoy + verb + *-ing* or noun

When you use *like, love, hate* and *enjoy* with a verb,
use the verb + *-ing.*
Examples:
I like running every morning.
He loves going to the beach.
We hate seafood.
They enjoy travelling.
Why don't you like the new office?
What do they enjoy doing in their free time?
I hate working weekends.
She enjoys football.

Unit 4

there is / there are

Full form	Questions	Short answers
Positive There's ... There are ...	Is there ...?	Yes, there is. No, there isn't.
Negative There isn't ... There aren't ..	Are there ...?	Yes, there are. No, there aren't.

Use *there's* to talk about singular nouns.
Use *there are* to talk about plural nouns.
Examples:
There's a park.
There are some nice shops.

There is / are + determiner

Full form	Questions	Short answers
Positive There's a / an ... There are some...	Is there a / an ...?	Yes, there is. No, there isn't.
Negative There isn't a / an ... There aren't any ...	Are there any ...?	Yes, there are. No, there aren't.

Is there a bureau de change in the town centre?
No, there isn't a bureau de change, but there's a bank.
Are there any good restaurants near here?
No, there aren't any restaurants, but there's a nice café near here.

Note:
Use *a / an* in positive sentences, negative sentences and questions with *there is*.
Use *some* in positive sentences.
Use *any* in negative sentences and questions.

Comparative and superlative

		Adjective	Comparative	Superlative
Most one-syllable adjectives	+ *er / est*	cold	colder	the coldest
One-syllable adjectives ending in -*e*	+ *r / st*	late	later	the latest
One- and two-syllable adjectives ending in consonant + *y*	*y* + *ier / iest*	pretty	prettier	the prettiest
One-syllable adjectives ending in one vowel + one consonant (except -*y*, -*w*)	double consonant	fat	fatter	the fattest
Adjectives of two or more syllables	*more / the most* (or *less / least*) + + adjective	beautiful	more beautiful	the most beautiful
Irregulars		good bad far	better worse farther / further	the best the worst the farthest / furthest

Comparative adjectives
a) Use comparative adjective + *than* to compare people or things.
Examples:
John's older than Jeanette.
Canada's bigger than the USA.
b) Use *a lot / much / far* or *a bit / a little* before comparative adjectives.
Examples:
Your work's much better than mine.
That book's a bit more boring than this one.
c) Compare quantity using *more / less* + uncountable noun or *more / fewer* + countable noun.
Examples:
Pasta has more calories than salad.
There are fewer potatoes on my plate than on yours.
Note:
In formal English, say:
Gary is taller than I am / than she is.
In conversational English, we usually say:
Gary's taller than me / than her.

Superlative adjectives
a) Use *the* + superlative adjective to compare a person or thing with everyone / thing else in a particular group.
Example:
John's the oldest (person) in the group.
b) We usually put *in* before the names of places or groups of people. In most other cases, use *of* after superlatives.
Examples:
Madrid's the biggest city in Spain.
I'm the youngest of three boys.
c) Use *by far* before superlative adjectives for emphasis.
Example:
That was by far the best party this year.
d) Compare quantity using *the most / the least* + uncountable noun or the *most / the fewest* + countable noun.
Example:
Of all my friends, Sue has the least money.

Unit 5

Countable and uncountable – *a/an, some* and *any*

Use *a* and *an* with one object.
Examples:
a telephone, an umbrella
Use *some* with plural countable nouns and uncountable nouns.
We usually use *some* in positive sentences.
Examples:
some food, some water, some clothes

	Singular	Plural
Countable nouns	**a/an** a restaurant an egg	**some** some restaurants some eggs
Uncountable nouns	**some** some coffee some bread	

Use *any* in negative sentences and questions.
Examples:
Are there any brochures in that box?
No, there aren't any in the box, but there are some on the table.
Is there any milk in the fridge?
No, there isn't.

Use *some* when we ask for something in particular, or when we offer something in particular.
Examples:
Can I have some coffee?
Would you like some biscuits?

Much, many and *a lot of*

Use quantifiers to talk about quantity:
How much milk do we have?
How many people work nights?
She doesn't have much information.
They don't have many computers.

Uncountable nouns	How much (information)?
Countable nouns	How many (cars)?
Uncountable & countable nouns	a lot of / lots of / some (coffee / phones)

Use *many* for negatives and questions with countable nouns.
Use *many* in positive sentences.
Use *much* for negatives and questions with uncountable nouns.
Use a *lot of* for positive sentence with both countable and uncountable nouns.

I'd like, I like

Don't confuse *like* + noun or *-ing* form and *would like* + noun or *would like to* + infinitive.
Examples:

They like seafood. (= they enjoy it)
I like reading. (= I enjoy it)
I'd like to read tonight. (= I want to do it)
We'd like some coffee. (= we want to drink some coffee and not, for example, some tea)

Questions:
Would you like some milk?
Do you like milk?

Unit 6

Present continuous

Full form	Questions	Short answers
Positive I'm working. You / We / They're working. He / She / It's working.	Am I working? Are you / we / they working? are. Is he / she / it working?	Yes, I am. Yes, they No, she isn't.
Negative I'm not working. You / We / They aren't working. He / She / It isn't working.		

Note:
These are the full forms of the positive and negative verbs.
I am working.
You / We / They are working.
He / She / It is working.
I am not working.
You / We / They are not working.
He / She / It isn't working.

Only use these full forms:
a) in formal writing.
b) for emphasis.

Use the present continuous to describe temporary activities.
Examples:
The trains aren't running this week.
We aren't taking the bus today.
Are you cycling to work this morning?

Use the present continuous to talk about what you're doing at the moment.
Examples:
What are you doing?
I'm watching a film.

Use time expressions like *at the moment*, *today* and *now* with the present continuous.

Spelling rules for *-ing* verbs
1   With most verbs, simply add *-ing* to the verb.
    Examples:
    do – doing, read – reading, walk – walking
2   When a verb has one syllable and ends with a consonant–vowel–consonant combination, double the last consonant and add *-ing* to the verb.
    Examples:
    run – running, put – putting, swim – swimming
3   When the verb ends in an *-e*, drop the *-e* and add *-ing* to   the verb.
    Examples:
    have – having, take – taking, come – coming

Present continuous – future arrangements

Use the present continuous to talk about the future.
Example:
What are you doing next weekend?
I'm going to the beach.

Use the present continuous to talk about plans and arrangements in the future which are sure to happen.
Often there is a definite time and / or place for arrangements in the present continuous.
Example:
I'm catching the 6 p.m. train tomorrow.

Unit 7

Past simple – be

The past of the verb be has two forms: was and were.

Full form	Questions	Short answers
Positive I / He / She / It was happy. You / We / They were happy. **Negative** I / He / She / It wasn't happy. You / We / They weren't happy.	Was I / he / she / it happy? Were you / we / they happy?	Yes, I / he / she / it was. No, I / he / she / it wasn't. Yes, you / we / they were. No, you / we / they weren't.

Note:

These are the full forms of the negative verbs and the negative short answer.

I / He / She / It was not very happy.
You / We / They were not very happy.
No, I / he / she / it was not.
No, you / we / they were not.

Only use these full forms:
a) in formal writing.
b) for emphasis.

Past simple – regular forms

Full form	Questions	Short answers
Positive I / You / He / She / It / We / They worked. **Negative** I / You / He / She / It / We / They didn't work.	Did I / you / he / she / it / we / they work?	Yes, I / you / he / she / it / we / they did. No, I / you / he / she / it / we / they didn't.

Note:

These are the full forms of the negative verbs and the negative short answer.

I / You / He / She / It / We / They did not work.
No, I / you / he / she / it / we / they did not.
Only use these full forms:
a) in formal writing.
b) for emphasis.

Use the past simple to talk about events that happened in the past.

Spelling rules for regular past simple verbs
Most of the spelling rules for -ed are the same as for -ing. There is one additional rule. When a verb ends in a consonant + y, drop the y, add an i and then add ed.
Example:
try – tried

Past simple – irregular forms

Some past simple verbs are irregular and they have an irregular past simple form.
Examples:
go – went, have – had.

Full form	Questions	Short answers
Positive I / You / He / She / It / We / They went to the mountains. **Negative** I / You / He / She / It / We / They didn't go to the mountains.	Did I / you / he / she / it / we / they go to the mountains?	Yes, I / you / he / she / it / we / they did No, I / you / he / she / it / we / they didn

Note:

These are the full forms of the negative verbs and the negative short answer.

I / You / He / She / It / We / They did not work.
No, I / you / he / she / it / we / they did not.

Only use these full forms:
a) in formal writing.
b) for emphasis.

The verb can is a special case. The past simple of can is could. We form the negative with couldn't.
Example:
He could ride a bike, but he couldn't drive a car.

The past of have or has is had.
The past of get is got.
The past of do or does is did.

See the list of irregular verbs on page 110.

Unit 8

Past simple

See Unit 7

Unit 9

Modal verbs

have to / don't have to

Full form	Questions	Short answers
Positive I / You / He / She / It / We / They have to	Do I / you / he / she / it / we / they have to?	Yes, I / you / he / she / it / we / they do.
Negative I / You / He / She / It / We / They don't have to		No, I / you / he / she / it / we / they don't.

Use *have to* to say that something is necessary.
Example:
I have to wear a uniform to work.
Use *don't have to* to say that something isn't necessary.
Example:
You don't have to do it if you don't want to.

can / can't

Full form	Questions	Short answers
Positive I / You / He / She / It / We / They can go	Can I / you / he / she / it / we / they go?	Yes, I / you / he / she / it / we / they can.
Negative I / You / He / She / It / We / They can't go		No, I / you / he / she / it / we / they can't.

Use *can't* to say that something is not allowed.
Example:
You can't park your car here.

Note:

Can does not have an infinitive or a past participle (NOT ~~to can~~ / ~~I've canned~~). Instead, use (*to*) *be able to* and *been able to*.
a) We use *can* when we mean 'you are able' or 'you are permitted'.
Example:
You can leave school at the age of sixteen in the UK.

b) We also use *can* to ask for permission.
Example:
Can I borrow your pen?
c) We use *can't* when we mean 'you are not able' or 'you are not permitted'.
Example:
You can't get married – you're only fifteen.

Unit 10

will for decisions and promises

Use *will* + infinitive to make decisions.
These can be:
a) offers of help.
Example:
I'll do you a favour.
b) promises.
Example:
I'll give you the money next week. (NOT I ~~give you~~ ...)

c) refusals.
Example:
I won't help him again.
d) orders of food and drink.
Example:
I'll have the tomato soup, please.
e) spontaneous (unplanned) decisions or decisions made at the moment of speaking.
Example:
(the phone rings) I'll answer it.

Irregular verbs

Infinitive	Past simple	Past participle
be	was, were	been
become	became	become
begin	began	begun
bite	bit	bitten
break	broke	broken
bring	brought	brought
build	built	built
buy	bought	bought
catch	caught	caught
choose	chose	chosen
come	came	come
cost	cost	cost
do	did	done
dream	dreamt/dreamed	dreamt/dreamed
drink	drank	drunk
drive	drove	driven
eat	ate	eaten
fall	fell	fallen
feel	felt	felt
fight	fought	fought
find	found	found
fly	flew	flown
forbid	forbade	forbidden
forget	forgot	forgotten
forgive	forgave	forgiven
get	got	got/gotten (US)
give	gave	given
go	went	gone
grow	grew	grown
have	had	had
hear	heard	heard
hide	hid	hidden
hit	hit	hit
hold	held	held
hurt	hurt	hurt
keep	kept	kept
know	knew	known
lead	led	led
learn	learnt/learned	learnt/learned
leave	left	left
let	let	let
light	lit	lit
lose	lost	lost
make	made	made
meet	met	met
pay	paid	paid

Infinitive	Past simple	Past participle
put	put	put
read /riːd/	read /red/	read /red/
ride	rode	ridden
ring	rang	rung
rise	rose	risen
run	ran	run
say	said	said
see	saw	seen
sell	sold	sold
send	sent	sent
set	set	set
shake	shook	shaken
shoot	shot	shot
show	showed	shown/showed
shut	shut	shut
sing	sang	sung
sit	sat	sat
sleep	slept	slept
smell	smelt/smelled	smelt/smelled
speak	spoke	spoken
spend	spent	spent
spill	spilt/spilled	spilt/spilled
spread	spread	spread
stand	stood	stood
steal	stole	stolen
stick	stuck	stuck
stink	stank/stunk	stunk
strike	struck	struck
swear	swore	sworn
sweep	swept	swept
swell	swelled	swollen/swelled
swim	swam	swum
swing	swung	swung
take	took	taken
teach	taught	taught
tear	tore	torn
tell	told	told
think	thought	thought
throw	threw	thrown
understand	understood	understood
upset	upset	upset
wake	woke	woken
wear	wore	worn
weep	wept	wept
wet	wet/wetted	wet/wetted
win	won	won
write	wrote	written

Functional language

Unit 1

Greetings and goodbyes

Hi

Hello

Good morning

How are you?

See you soon

Bye

Goodbye

Have a safe journey

Exchanging contact details

What's your phone / mobile number?

What's the (area) code?

What's your extension?

Unit 2

Answering the phone

Good morning / afternoon, (Pavilion Ltd). (Katia) speaking. How can I help?

Asking for someone

Can I speak to (Robert Kott), please?

Asking who's calling

May I ask who's calling?

Saying who you are

It's (Thomas Freund) from (Terco).

Saying if someone isn't there

I'm sorry, he's in a meeting.

I'm afraid he's on holiday this week.

Offering to take a message

Can I take a message?

Taking someone's number

Can I take your number?

Unit 3

Ordering and paying for food

I'd like (a large box of sushi), please.

Could I / we have (a soup of the day), please?

To have here or take away?

Could I have the bill now, please?

Unit 4

Booking a hotel

I'd like to make a reservation for (four nights) from (the fourth of February), please.

What kind of room would you like?

I'd like a single / double room.

Could you tell me the room rate, please?

Does that include breakfast?

OK, we'll take it.

Unit 5

Opinions and offers

Would you like (a coffee)?

Yes, please. / No, thanks. I don't drink coffee.

How would you like your coffee?

White, with two sugars, please. / Black, no sugar, thanks.

Do you like (spicy food)?

Yes. I love it! / No, it's not my favourite.

Could I have an aisle seat?

Requests

I'd like (a table for two), please.

Could we have (a table for four), please?

Could you (pass the water), please?

Unit 6

Air travel

Can I have your passport, please?

How many bags do you have?

Could you put it on the scales for me, please?

Could I have an aisle seat?

Train travel

What time does the (14.15) arrive?

Could I get a ticket for that train, please?

Can you tell me which platform (the 12.05 to Naples) departs from?

Could I have a single / return to (Brussels), please?

Unit 7
Shopping

How can I help you?

Do you need any help?

What is it you're looking for?

How many would you like?

How would you like to pay?

Is there anything else?

Is there (a café) near here?

Which floor are (bags) on?

Which floor is that on?

Can I have one of those, please?

Do you have any (pens)?

How much are they?

Do you take credit cards?

Unit 8
Meetings

Shall we …?

How about …?

I think …

I'm not sure …

I agree.

Definitely, without doubt.

I see what you mean, but …

I don't know about that.

Unit 9
Emails

Dear Mr Campbell

Dear Sir

Dear Colin

Hi Colin

Yours sincerely

Best wishes / Best regards

All the best

Cheers

I attach … / Please find attached …

Can you … / I would be grateful if you could …

It will be great to see you again. / I look forward to seeing you again.

Unit 10
Suggestions

Shall we (go out for dinner tonight)?

What shall we do (for lunch)?

We / You can / could …

Why don't we …

Let's …

Offers

Would you like me to …

Shall I …?

Can I …?

I'll …

Yes, that's a good idea.

Yes, I agree.

Excellent idea!

No, I don't think so.

No, I'm afraid I …

Sorry, but I'm not sure …

Audioscripts

Unit 1

))) 1.1

Sydney

This is Karen Wood. She's 43 years old. She's an engineer for Alsthom in Sydney, Australia. She's married. Her husband's a software designer. His name's Sanjit. He's from Pune in India.

Osaka

This is Yuji Kamasaki. He's 29 years old and he's a sales representative for Nissan. He's single. He works at the Nissan offices in Osaka in the south of Japan, but Yuji's originally from the north of the country. His hometown's Morioka.

Montevideo

This is Santiago Ramos and this is Rosa Perez. They're from Montevideo and they're both computer programmers for Microsoft Uruguay. They're married and their partners also work for Microsoft. Rosa's husband is an administrator and Santiago's wife is a director.

))) 1.2

O = officer, S = Santiago

O: Now, can I ask you some questions, please, sir? I just need to complete your registration form.
S: Of course.
O: So, what's your surname, please?
S: I'm sorry … could you say that again?
O: What's your surname, your family name?
S: Oh, I understand … it's Ramos. And my first name is Santiago.
O: Thank you, sir. And where are you from?
S: I arrived today from Montevideo, but I'm actually from Mexico. I have a Mexican passport.
O: Thank you, sir. OK – and what's your date of birth?
S: 18th October 1976.
O: What's your job?
S: I'm a computer programmer. I work for Microsoft.
O: OK, thank you and one last question. Can I have your home address, please?
S: Yes. It's Calle …

))) 1.3

1 I'm from Brazil.
2 They're from Australia.
3 I'm a manager.
4 We're American.
5 She's a software engineer.
6 It's in Australia.

))) 1.4

S = Santiago, C = Chintal, R = Rosa

S: Hello, Chintal! I saw your name on the list. How are you?
C: Santiago! What a surprise! How good to see you! But what are you doing here?
S: I'm here for the conference of course, and this is my colleague, Rosa Perez. We work together in Montevideo. Rosa, this is my old friend Chintal Patel from Sydney. We were at university together. He's a software designer with Dell.
R: Hello, Chintal, nice to meet you.
C: Hello, Rosa, good to meet you, too.

))) 1.5

1 Spain
2 Britain, British, China, German, Spanish
3 Brazil, Chinese, Japan
4 Germany, India, Indian, Mexico, Mexican, Portugal
5 Japanese, Portuguese
6 America, American, Brazilian

))) 1.6

1

R = receptionist, C = customer

R: Good evening, sir. Can I help you?
C: Good evening. Yes, I have a reservation.
R: What's your name, please?
C: Manuel Azevedo.
R: Is that a Spanish name?
C: No, it isn't Spanish. It's Portuguese.

2

P = passport officer, T = traveller

P: Could I see your passport and visa please, madam?
T: Here they are.
P: Are you here on holiday?
T: No, we aren't. We're here for a conference.
P: And where are you staying?
T: The Pacific International Hotel on Palm Avenue.
P: Thank you. Enjoy your stay.

3

R = receptionist, C = customer

R: Good morning, LSG, Lily speaking. How can I help you?
C: Hello. Could I speak to Wayne Zheng, please?
R: I'm sorry, who?
C: Wayne Zheng.
R: Which department is he in, please?
C: He's in the sales department.
R: One moment, please … I'm sorry, he isn't at his desk at the moment. Can I take a message?

))) 1.7

a b c d e f g h i j k l m n o p q r s t u v w x y z

))) 1.8

a h j k
b c d e g p t v
f l m n s x z
i y
o
q u w
r

))) 1.9

1 My boss's name is Lara Alexander. That's L-A-R-A, Lara and A-L-E-X-A-N-D-E-R, Alexander.
2 My hometown's a small town in Western Ukraine called Berezhany – B-E-R-E-Z-H-A-N-Y. Do you want me to spell it again? B-E-R-E-Z-H-A-N-Y.
3 The person you want to speak to is Sophie Perret. That's Sophie S-O-P-H-I-E, Perret, P-E double R (two Rs) E-T.
4 The hotel address is 32 – three two – Kirova Street. Yes, Kirova, K-I-R-O-V-A.

5   Yes, it's out in the desert in Saudi Arabia. The nearest town is called Aba ar Ruwath. That's three words: Aba capital A-B-A, then ar, A-R, and the last word is Ruwath, R-U-W-A-T-H.

6   The new CEO is American. His name's Daniel Cohen. That's Daniel – D-A-N-I-E-L, Cohen – C-O-H-E-N.

1.10

1
A: Hello. Good morning, everybody.
B: Hello, Mrs Kim. Nice to see you again.

2
A: Bye then, and thanks for everything.
B: Bye, Sally, see you soon.

3
A: Goodbye.
B: Thank you for meeting us today.
A: You're welcome.
C: Have a safe journey. Thank you for coming.

4
A: Hi, Leandro, how are you?
B: Fine, thanks. And you?
A: I'm fine.

1.11

0 1 2 3 4 5 6 7 8 9 10 11 12 13 14 15 16 17 18 19 20 21 22 23 24 25 26 27 28 29 30 40 50 60 70 80 90 100

1.12

13
50

1.13

1   90
2   80
3   17
4   16
5   50
6   14
7   30

1.14

1
A: Sorry, Sally, I'm very busy. Can I call you back later? What's your mobile number?
B: It's 07995 436 779.
A: Great. Speak to you later.

2
A: I think it's a wrong number. What's the area code for Cologne?
B: It's 0221.

3
A: I need to ring Pablo.
B: He's in Mexico now.
A: What's the code for Mexico?
B: It's 0052.

4
A: Can I call you later?
B: Sure.
A: What's your extension?
B: It's 7224.

1.15

r.juszko_05@gmail.com
andrea.szabo@inco.hu
swan_julia@aol.com

1.16

1   t.glock_9@gmail.com
2   l_b.roberts.8@hotmail.com
3   achau_16@yahoo.com
4   zhang_shen@google.com

1.17

Javier
Hi, Manal. Javier here. I want to try to meet someone called Henry Wu – that's W-U – at the conference. I think he works for Red Software, but I can't find him or the company on the internet. Do you know who I mean?

Manal
Hi Javier, just returning your call. I know a company called Red Dragon Software. I think he might work there.

Agna
Hi Javier, Manal said you want to meet Henry Wu. He's an excellent software programmer. His phone number is 0086 973 6559 and his email is h.wu@yahoo.com.

1.18

A = Agna, **M** = Manal, **J** = Javier
A: Hi, Manal. How are you?
M: Fine thanks, Agna.
A: Manal, this is Javier.
J: Pleased to meet you.
M: Pleased to meet you, too.
J: Where are you from?
M: I'm from Lebanon, and you?
J: I'm from Spain. Is Henry here?
A: No, he isn't. His email and mobile aren't working.
J: Let me see? That is his mobile number, but that isn't his email. His email is h_wu@yahoo.com.
M: That isn't his number. I called and someone else answered. Is that the code for China?
J: Yes, it is.

1.19

A = Agna, **R** = receptionist
A: Hello. We need to speak to Mr Wu, Mr Henry Wu. Could you ring him, please?
R: We have two Mr Wus staying with us. There's a Mr H Wu in room 18 and also another Mr H Wu in room 80.
A: We think his mobile number is 07786 521 10.
R: Let me see … that isn't the mobile number for Mr Wu in room 18 … and I'm sorry, it isn't the number for the Mr Wu in room 80 either. Do you know his first name?
A: Yes, it's Henry.
R: OK, then he's in room 80.

Unit 2

2.1

Waiter
I live in Portugal in the capital city, Lisbon. I live in a small apartment in the historic centre. I don't work in the centre of Lisbon. I work in a restaurant in another part of town. I take people's orders and serve drinks and food to the tables. I go to work by tram and boat because the restaurant where I work is on the other side of the river. I earn €12,000 a year.

Customer service representative
I live in a large flat in Muscat, Oman. I'm married and I have four children. My parents also live with us in the flat. I have a car and I go to work in my car. I don't work in an office. I sell

products, but I also answer questions and deal with complaints. I work long days and finish work at 8.00 p.m. I earn RO1,200 per month.

))) 2.2

Hotel manager

I live in a flat in Hong Kong. I'm married and I have one child. I work in a hotel in Kowloon; I'm the general manager. I go to work on the underground every day. I don't work normal hours every day. My hours and days are different every week. I earn one million Hong Kong dollars a year.

))) 2.3

Monday
Tuesday
Wednesday
Thursday
Friday
Saturday
Sunday

))) 2.4

January
February
March
April
May
June
July
August
September
October
November
December
spring
summer
autumn
winter

))) 2.5

1

I = interviewer, **S** = Saud

I: Do you work every day, Saud?
S: Not on a Friday. It's our religious day. Many people only have a day off on Friday. I'm lucky – I get Thursday and Friday free.
I: How much holiday do you get?
S: I get 30 days' holiday and another nine days for religious and national days.
I: When do you take your holidays?
S: The national day is in September. Ramadan is different every year. This year, it's in June. There are two seasons in Saudi Arabia – winter and summer. The summer's very hot so I often go to Europe.

2

I = interviewer, **A** = Ali

I: When are your days off, Ali?
A: I work Monday and Tuesday and have Wednesday off. I then work Thursday, Friday and Saturday and have Sunday off.
I: How much holiday do you get?
A: I get twenty-eight days' holiday. We can't take holidays in the summer.
I: When do you take your holiday?
A: I take my holidays before and after the busy period, often in spring and autumn. Christmas holidays are in December and in January, it's Australia Day. I stay in Australia for my holidays.

))) 2.6

1

R = receptionist, **C** = Carla

R: Good afternoon, Pavilion Ltd. Katia speaking. How can I help?
C: Good afternoon. Can I speak to Steven Pilkington, please?
R: May I ask who's calling?
C: It's Carla Carlson.
R: One moment, please. I'll just put you through.

2

R = receptionist, **T** = Thomas

R: Good morning, Key Stage Solutions. Steffan speaking. How can I help?
T: Can I speak to Robert Kott, please?
R: May I ask who's calling?
T: It's Thomas Freund from Terco.
R: I'm sorry, he's in a meeting. Can I take a message?
T: Yes, could you ask him to call me, please?
R: Can I take your number?
T: Yes, it's 01568 929 356.
R: Thank you. I'll leave a message for him.
T: Thank you. Goodbye.
R: Goodbye.

))) 2.7

00 / 44 / 60 / 9086
1 00 / 49 / 221 / 854
2 01582 / 587 / 924
3 07993 / 639 / 21

))) 2.8

1 0039 874 112
2 01289 326 859
3 9658 924
4 9664 711

))) 2.9

1 chair
2 coffee cup
3 desk
4 keyboard
5 laptop screen
6 pen
7 pencil
8 photo of my dog
9 plant
10 window

))) 2.10

C = Constantinos, **H** = Hazel

C: OK, well, great, we have the new person, but now we have three people and two desks.
H: Yes, let's look at each of them. So first, Manos.
C: Yes, he works Monday to Friday. Five days a week.
H: He also works from 9 to 5 every day.
C: He does, but he's out of the office three days of the week.
H: When's he out of the office? He's out on Monday, Tuesday and Thursday.
C: He also has a meeting for the whole afternoon every Wednesday.
H: OK, so let's talk about Gizem.
C: Well, she only works Monday to Thursday. And she likes to work from 8 to 4.
H: She also visits customers on Tuesday and Wednesday.
C: So she needs the desk on Monday and Thursday?

H: Yes, but I think she can use another room on Thursday morning.
C: Why?
H: She makes a lot of calls. They're usually meetings on Skype.
C: So she can use the meeting room on Thursday morning.
H: OK, finally Emel. She works four days a week.
C: What days does she work?
H: She works Tuesday to Friday.
C: What hours does she work?
H: She works from 10 to 6 most days. But she visits customers on Wednesday, Thursday and Friday mornings.
C: Does she have any meetings?
H: On Friday afternoons, she has a sales meeting.

Unit 3

3.1
1
does
reads
means
calms
handles
needs
2
thinks
looks
hates
asks
3
finishes
fixes
organises

3.2
a nine o'clock
b half past six
c eight o'clock
d half past eight
e quarter past eleven
f quarter to three

3.3
a ten o'clock
b quarter past two
c quarter to four
d twelve o'clock
e eleven thirty
f quarter past nine

3.4
Valentina
My name's Valentina and I live in Rosario in Argentina. I'm very busy in the week. I'm a marketing manager in a big IT company and I always work long hours. Sometimes I don't get home until 10.00 p.m. Because I'm so busy during the week, at the weekends I try to catch up on my sleep. When I finally get up, I like doing sport with my husband. We usually go running together. After that we often eat out for lunch – there's a great Italian restaurant five minutes from our flat. I love eating good food, but I hardly ever cook – I'm terrible at it. Luckily my husband's a great cook.

Matt
My name's Matt and I'm a student at Oxford University. I study hard during the week, but I try to have one or two hours free every evening. I usually surf the net for an hour. I like reading football news – my favourite team is Manchester United so there's always a lot to read. Then I often watch TV – I like watching the news or comedy shows. I hate watching soap operas – the stories are stupid and I find them really boring, but my housemate loves them. When she watches them, I always go to my bedroom to study.

Katerina
My name's Katerina. I live in Warsaw in Poland. I work in a bank and I don't like my job. It's really boring – but luckily I like my work colleagues and we do a lot of things together in the evenings. I love going out to restaurants, bars and nightclubs mainly because I like to spend time with other people. Every Wednesday, I go out for a meal with three friends from work. We all love eating out. I really love dancing in nightclubs too, so we usually go to a club after dinner. At the weekends, I see my family. Me and my younger brother love playing computer games and listening to music so we spend a lot of time doing that at our parents' house.

3.5
1 I don't like a big lunch, so I usually just have a bowl of soup or a salad.
2 I love Asian food, so I often have sushi, or sometimes I buy a bento box.
3 I'm typically English. It's sandwiches every day! And a cup of tea afterwards, of course.
4 Normally I take lunch to work, but on Fridays I always have steak and chips with my colleagues.
5 I go home and have lunch with my wife. We usually have curry with rice and a cup of coffee afterwards.

3.6
1 a cup of tea
2 a cup of coffee
3 a bowl of soup
4 steak and chips
5 We usually have
6 typically English

3.7
a 20
b 13
c 140
d 115
e 63
f 217
g 80
h 190
i 48

3.8
a €10.20
b $12.50
c £15.99
d £29.99
e €50.15
f $66.76
g €14.40
h $89
i $5.25
j €17.87

)) 3.9

1
A: I'd like a large box of sushi, please.
B: OK. That's four dollars fifteen, please.

2
A: Could I have a small soup of the day and a side salad, please?
B: Right, that'll be five euros fifty, then.

3
A: Could I have a chicken sandwich, please – and a coke?
B: That's five dollars seventeen.

4
A: Two portions of vegetable curry with rice and two glasses of water.
B: Very good, sir. That will be twelve euros sixty-six, please.

5
A: Could we have four portions of steak and chips and four cups of tea, please?
B: Four portions of steak and chips and four teas? Let me see –that's thirty dollars exactly.

)) 3.10

1
Ca = café worker, **Cu** = customer
Ca: Good morning. What can I get you?
Cu: Hi. I'd like an Americano, please.
Ca: Certainly. Regular or large?
Cu: Large, please.
Ca: To have here or take away?
Cu: Take away, please.
Ca: Here you are. That's one dollar, sixty-five … Thank you. Have a nice day.
Cu: Thank you. And you. Bye.

2
W = waiter, **C** = customer
W: Hello, madam. Are you ready to order?
C: Yes, please. I'll have the soup and a sandwich, please.
W: Anything to drink with that?
C: Er, yes. Could I have a coke, please?

3
W = waiter, **C** = customer
W: Anything for dessert?
C: I don't think so, thank you … Could I have the bill now, please?
W: Certainly, madam.

)) 3.11

Hi, Nick. This is Sven. I'm not in the office tomorrow, so can you do some things for me? First I need you to arrange a meeting for Monday with Helen. It's really important you do this first thing as she's very busy and her schedule is very full. Could you also telephone head office to ask Katia to come to the meeting? I won't be able to make lunch with Giancarlo so you'll have to go. Make sure it goes well because he's an important customer. After you finish lunch, there's a report on your desk to read. Check you agree with it and then send it to head office. And don't forget you're writing the accounts report for me. You'll need the whole afternoon to write it, but I want it on Monday.

)) 3.12

N = Nick, **V** = Viviana
N: Hi, Viviana, it's Nick.
V: Hi, Nick. How are you?
N: Good, but I have too much work.
V: You always have too much work!
N: I know, I know. Can you help me?
V: With work?!
N: No, no. Can you buy Mum a birthday present for me?
V: What?! It's her birthday on Monday.
N: I know. I have to work this lunchtime and I'm not here at the weekend.
V: You can come out on Monday night though, can't you?
N: Yes, don't worry, I can.
V: You have to or Mum will kill you!

)) 3.13

W = waitress, **N** = Nick, **G** = Giancarlo
W: Have you decided what you'd like yet?
N: I think so. Giancarlo?
G: Yes, I'm ready.
N: Could I have a pizza and side salad?
W: Sure. Anything to drink?
N: A coke, please.
W: And for you, sir?
G: I'll have a steak and chips, please, and a bottle of water.
W: OK. So that's one pizza and a side salad and one steak and chips – and one coke and one water.

)) 3.14

N = Nick, **G** = Giancarlo
N: So, do you have any nice plans for the weekend?
G: Nothing exciting – probably just the usual.
N: What do you usually do?
G: I try to do some exercise every Saturday morning and I really like cycling. Then in the afternoon, I like relaxing watching the football on TV. In the evening, I enjoy cooking a nice meal with my partner. What about you?
N: Quite similar really. I also try to exercise in the morning and I like playing tennis. If the weather's nice, I stay in the park and relax with a book. But I'm afraid I'm a bit lazy with the cooking and really enjoy eating out.

)) 3.15

N = Nick, **G** = Giancarlo, **W** = waitress
N: How's your food?
G: The steak's good, but the chips are cold.
N: Yes, so's my pizza.
G: Can we send them back?
N: I'm sorry. I don't think we have time. I think your next meeting is at half past two. Let's have a coffee instead. Excuse me! Two coffees, please.
W: I'm sorry sir, we've run out of coffee.
N: Oh … OK. Can I have the bill, please?
W: Here you are, sir.
N: Do you take credit cards?
W: I'm sorry sir, not today. The machine is broken.
N: Oh … I don't have any money with me … Er, Giancarlo, could you …?

•))) **3.16**

Hello Nick

How are you, my dear? I know you're working very hard at the moment, poor boy. I'm phoning to say don't forget our plans for my birthday this evening. We're meeting outside the theatre at seven o'clock. I'm looking forward to it so much – I love Shakespeare!

See you this evening at 7.00.

Bye!

Unit 4

•))) **4.1**

1

D = Diana, **R** = receptionist

D: Hi, could you tell me, is there a good restaurant near here?

R: There are lots of good restaurants. We're on Riu da Quitanda – here on this map. If you go out of the hotel and turn right, go straight on until the crossroads and then turn right. You'll be on Riu Sete de Setembro. There are lots of good restaurants along there.

D: Are there any Mexican restaurants there?

R: I don't think there are any Mexican restaurants. There's a Japanese restaurant on the right. Opposite there's a Brazilian restaurant and next to that there's an Italian restaurant.

D: Which is the best one? I'm taking an important client out for dinner.

R: The Brazilian restaurant is really good and very popular.

D: Great, thank you.

2

L = Leandro, **D** = Diana

L: So is everything OK with your trip?

D: Excellent, thank you. Our meetings have been really productive.

L: Is there anything you need at all?

D: Actually, is there a pharmacy near here? I need to buy some contact lens solution.

L: There isn't one near here, but there is one very near your hotel. When you go out of your hotel, turn left and go straight on. After 500 metres, there's a small pharmacy on your left.

3

D = Diana, **P** = person in the street

D: Hi, sorry, is there a phone shop near here?

P: There's one next to the old cathedral. Keep going straight along here until the end of the street. At the junction, turn left and go straight on for three or four minutes. The cathedral is in front of you and on the left is a phone shop.

D: Great, thank you. Do they sell SIM cards I can put in my American phone?

P: I think so, but there's also another shop behind the cathedral so you can also try there.

4

D = Diana, **P** = person in the street

D: Is there a taxi rank near here?

P: There isn't a taxi rank, but there are lots of taxis on Avenida Rodrigues Alves. Go left here and go straight on until you get to the traffic lights. Turn right and go straight on and it's the road at the end of the street.

D: Is it far? I need to get to the airport quickly – my flight leaves in two hours!

P: Take this bus. It goes to the airport and gets there in fifteen minutes.

D: Really? Brilliant! Thank you.

•))) **4.2**

1

Johannesburg is one of the biggest cities in South Africa. The city is famous for its gold mines and because it's the home of Nelson Mandela, the former South African president. According to a recent survey, it's the cheapest city in the world for foreigners to live in, because food and housing aren't expensive.

2

Many people think that Paris is one of the most beautiful and most romantic cities in the world and, with 30–40 million visitors a year, it's the most visited. Until the nineteenth century, this city was the biggest in Europe, but today with a population of 2.5 million, it's smaller than Berlin or London.

3

With a population of over 13 million, Tokyo is the biggest city in the world. It's an important global business centre. It's also one of the best places in the world to go shopping or eat out. There are more top-class restaurants in this city than Paris or New York.

4

This sea port in south-west China is the fastest growing city in the world. With its beautiful beaches and green parks, Beihai is prettier than Beijing or Shanghai and has more tourists. But it's also an important centre for trade and industry, including shipbuilding.

•))) **4.3**

Cristiano

I don't have much money so I need a cheap room. I don't have a car so I want to be near the city centre where the conference is. In the evenings, I like to relax and read a book. I don't need for there to be a restaurant in the hotel. I'm happy to eat anywhere that isn't too expensive.

Vera

I work long hours and my job is stressful so I need a good hotel with all the facilities. I get up early and work out for an hour, so I want a good gym with a pool. It's important that there's a good wireless internet connection so I can read my emails, and a business centre would be useful. I want a hotel with excellent restaurants so I can entertain my clients. Oh, and the hotel must be near the airport so I don't have to worry about catching my flight.

Simon and Laura

We've got small children so we need a family-friendly hotel preferably with parking so we don't have to carry the baby everywhere. We'd like to be near the beach, but also want the hotel to have a good swimming pool as well in case the weather isn't good. Although we love good food, we can't go out to eat in the evening because of the baby's bedtime, so we need decent room service.

•))) **4.4**
January
February
March
April
May
June
July
August
September
October
November
December

•))) **4.5**
1st
2nd
3rd
4th
5th
6th
7th
8th
9th
10th
11th
12th
13th
14th
15th
16th
17th
18th
19th
20th
21st
22nd
30th
31st

•))) **4.6**
7th August
28th September
3rd January
29th July

•))) **4.7**
1
R = receptionist, C = Cristiano
R: Good afternoon, Hotel Ronda. Julia speaking. How can I help?
C: I'd like to make a reservation for four nights from the fourth of February, please.
R: Certainly. That's from Monday the fourth to Thursday the eighth of February. Is that right?
C: Yes.
R: And what kind of room would you like?
C: I'd like a single room.
R: OK … Let me see. Yes, that's no problem.
C: Could you tell me the room rate, please?
R: That's €55 a night for a single room, including breakfast.

2
R = receptionist, L = Laura
R: Good morning, the Mirador Hotel. Maria speaking, how can I help?
L: Hello, I'd like to reserve a double room for six nights from the 25th August.
R: Certainly, madam. Could you wait a moment, please, while I check availability? … All our standard double rooms are taken, but we do have a premium double room available for those dates.
L: Could you tell me the room rate, please?
R: Our premium rooms are €120 per night, plus VAT.
L: And does that include breakfast?
R: Yes, it does.
L: OK, we'll take it.
R: Certainly, madam. So that's a premium double room from 25th to 31st August …

•))) **4.8**
C = Colin, P = Paula
C: So we need to book rooms for three people, then?
P: That's right: Ayman, Shan and Bruce.
C: What are their full names?
P: There's Ayman Lawati.
C: How do you spell that?
P: A-Y-M-A-N L-A-W-A-T-I. He's the Head of Marketing at ITS, our software partners in Bangalore.
C: Who's next?
P: Shan, that's S-H-A-N Wang W-A-N-G. She's the Finance Manager at the Washington office.
C: OK. So who's the last person again?
P: It's Bruce Darling.
C: Oh, yes, our new CEO.
P: That's right. He's the one we all have to impress.
C: So, can I leave it with you to book their rooms?
P: I'll need their arrival times and how long they're staying.
C: I'll just check my emails and let you know.

•))) **4.9**
Ayman
Hi there. It's Ayman from ITS in Bangalore. I'm just calling about my hotel booking. I need to ask you to book something that isn't too expensive. I've already had five trips this month so there isn't much money in my travel budget. I must have internet access in the room, and there must be breakfast included. The other meals are not important as I think you'll take us out, won't you?

Shan
Hi, Colin, it's Shan here. Just calling to talk about my visit next week. Thank you for offering to book my hotel. The price isn't important, but it must be excellent. You know I like high quality so make sure it is good. The rooms need to be very comfortable. I have a long flight and we have a lot of work to do so I must sleep well. I have to swim every morning so make sure there's a pool.

Bruce
Colin, it's Bruce. How are you? Hope you are well. Thank you for organising this trip. I'm really busy at the moment so it helps a lot. For the hotel, could you book something that's average cost? I like to get good quality, but for a good price – like in business! Make sure the hotel has at least four stars. Try to

book somewhere you know well, maybe somewhere you eat sometimes. Then you'll know what the customer service is like. I can stay in an average hotel when the customer service is excellent. I love a good view of the city so the higher the floor, the better!

Unit 5

·))) 5.1

Moussaka
It's a Greek dish. It's made of aubergines, lamb, tomatoes, garlic, lots of herbs and topped with cheese.

Brownie
It's a dessert. It's got lots of chocolate in it.

Steak
The steak is really good. It comes with potatoes, vegetables and a mushroom sauce.

Fish
The fish is baked in the oven and comes with salad. It's a starter, not a main course.

·))) 5.2

Different behaviour is polite in different countries. For example, in Japan, it's normal to pick up a bowl of soup and bring it to your mouth. In America, people hold their fork in the left hand. In the UK, it isn't polite to keep your elbows on the table, but in France, it's polite to do the same thing. In Saudi Arabia, people eat with their right hand. In El Salvador, you should leave a little food on the plate. In South Korea, talking isn't common during a meal.

·))) 5.3

1	Would you like a coffee?	No, thanks. I don't drink coffee.
2	Do you like spicy food?	Yes. I love it!
3	Would you like a slice of cake?	Yes, please.
4	Can I help you?	Yes, I'd like a table for two, please.
5	How's your dessert?	Good! I like cake, especially chocolate cake.

·))) 5.4

1	Could we have a table for four, please?	Certainly, is this one OK?
2	Would you like some more rice?	No thanks, I'm full.
3	Could you pass the water, please?	Of course. Here you are.
4	How would you like your coffee?	White, with two sugars, please.
5	Shall we split the bill?	No, it's my treat.
6	Could I have a glass of water, please?	Still or sparkling?

·))) 5.5

1 Could we have a table for four, please?
2 Would you like some more rice?
3 Could you pass the water, please?
4 How would you like your coffee?
5 Shall we split the bill?
6 Could I have a glass of water, please?

·))) 5.6

1
M = Miguel, **T** = Tom
M: It's so cold!
T: Really? This is nice compared to last week!
M: At the moment, it's 45 degrees in Madrid.
T: How do you work in that heat?
M: Every office has air-conditioning, so does my car and so does my house!
T: So we spend money making everything hot and you spend money making everything cold.
M: Crazy, isn't it? Are you ready to order?

2
M: So you call it soccer here?
T: Yes, and it's not very popular. Of course everyone knows the most famous players, but it's not even one of the top sports.
M: Which sports are?
T: Baseball, basketball, ice hockey and American football are all more popular.
M: Some people like basketball in my country, but football's much more popular. Do you play any sports?
T: I play basketball with my son and I'm in a baseball team. How about you?
M: I actually like playing tennis mostly.

3
M: So you play basketball with your son?
T: Yes, every Saturday.
M: How are your family?
T: They're well. My son has his exams next week. How about yours?
M: My son wants to come to America to study.
T: Oh, where?
M: Here in New York.

4
T: How's the steak?
M: It's really nice. Perfectly cooked. How's the fish?
T: Excellent. Much better than the starter.
M: Yes, it wasn't a good start to serve cold vegetable soup!

·))) 5.7

A: How's your steak?
B: Not great. It's cooked well, but it's really poor quality.
A: The same with my fish. I don't think they buy fresh ingredients.
C: Do you know what you'd like to eat?
D: I really can't decide.
C: I know. There's a difference between a good choice and too much choice.
D: Exactly. How many different combinations of pizza are there?!
E: How long ago did we finish our starter?
F: Half an hour ago!
E: This is too much. I'm really hungry.
F: There are lots of people working here and they're friendly, but the service is really slow.
G: There might be a traditional oven, but this isn't traditional pizza.
H: But it says traditional home-made Italian cooking.
G: Does your mum cook a frozen pizza for dinner?!
H: It does taste like a pizza from the supermarket. It's a shame because the location's great.

J: I can't eat all this.

G: Yes, it's too big. It's quite nice, but just too much.

J: The whole place needs some work.

G: The menu's too big, the decoration's nice but too old, the staff are friendly but slow. It could be a good restaurant with some work.

))) 5.8

C = consultant, S = Salvatore

C: So this is your fifth year in business?

S: Yes, next year is my sixth year, but the business might not survive.

C: And you say you have how much debt?

S: Nearly $250,000.

C: OK! So you need things to change quickly!

S: Yes, the sooner the better.

C: Can I get some basic figures from you?

S: Sure. What would you like to know?

C: How many people work here?

S: Fourteen in total.

C: That seems like too many people for such a small restaurant.

S: I know, but most of the staff are my family and friends.

C: How much is your weekly salary bill?

S: It's $14,000.

C: OK, how much are the other costs for rent and bills?

S: It's about $5,000 for rent and bills. The weekly food bill is $4,000.

C: And how many customers do you get on an average night?

S: For lunch and dinner? It's not great, maybe 20 or 30 on a weekday and 55–65 on a weekend.

C: How much does each customer spend on average?

S: They spend around $50.

C: So you lose around $1,000 every week?!

S: That's right. That's why I need your help!

Unit 6

))) 6.1

Juan

I = interviewer, J = Juan

I: So Juan, can you drive?

J: I can drive a car and a scooter.

I: Which do you drive to work?

J: I don't. I don't like driving because the roads are too busy. There is a good bus that I take each day.

I: What do you like about the bus?

J: It's cheap and quick.

Ann

I = interviewer, A = Ann

I: The roads are really busy in this city.

A: They are. More and more people use cars and scooters now.

I: So how do you travel to work?

A: I ride my scooter to work. I don't like how busy the roads are, but I like how quick it is going by scooter.

Omar

I = interviewer, O = Omar

I: Is there any public transport in the city, Omar?

O: There are buses, but there is no underground. I don't like driving, but there isn't any choice.

I: How do you travel to work?

O: By car. I don't take the bus because it's small and slow. I like driving directly from home to work. It's too hot to walk here, especially in the summer.

Da Long

I = interviewer, D = Da Long

I: For such a big city, there aren't many cars on the roads.

D: That's because we have excellent public transport.

I: So you use the bus to go to work?

D: No, I take the underground. The bus is cheap, but I like the fact that the underground doesn't get slowed down by traffic. I don't like taking the bus because it can be slow stopping everywhere. Once I get to my stop, I walk to my office.

))) 6.2

Juan

Z = Zhang, J = Juan

Z: Where are you?

J: Sorry, I'm still at work.

Z: Why are you still there?

J: The meeting went on a long time.

Z: So you're leaving now?

J: No, I'm just writing an email and then I'll leave.

Ann

H = Helen, A = Ann

H: Where are you?

A: In the car. The traffic's really bad.

H: When will you be home?

A: I don't know. Nothing's moving. The man in the car next to me is sleeping! The woman behind me is eating her dinner.

H: Fantastic! Well, I'm going to have my dinner now. I'll see you later.

Omar

C = Chintel, O = Omar

C: Where are you?

O: I'm still at the station.

C: Why, what's happening?

O: No trains are leaving at the moment. There's a technical problem.

C: What are you doing?

O: I'm just eating a snack and reading the paper. Many people are taking the bus or walking, but I'm going to wait.

C: OK, let me know when the train leaves.

))) 6.3

Larry

I'm travelling to the Middle East next week and I have to be really organised. I'm visiting four cities in two weeks. We supply department stores in all the cities and I'm going to meet each manager and their team. I fly into Dubai, but I'm not stopping over. I'm changing to a flight to Jeddah. Jeddah is in Saudi Arabia and I need a visa to go there. I have a boarding pass for the flight to Jeddah already because I don't have much time. I want to go straight through. We fly out one hour after I land. To enter Saudi Arabia, they also need to know where I'm staying. I'm booking my hotel tonight. I arrive late so I need to book a late check-in. I'm taking a taxi to the hotel and I'm in Jeddah for two days and then I'm flying to Riyadh. I'm renting a car for the rest of the trip and we're going to Dammam and then to Bahrain. It's so far from Australia that it makes sense for me to go to as many places as possible because the trip's quite expensive. A company is booking my flights because it's so complicated. I'm flying home after two weeks. I'm going to be very tired!

))) 6.4

1 She's working in London next week.
2 The bus is leaving at 10 o'clock.
3 My flight's leaving at 8 o'clock.
4 George's flying to Shanghai on Sunday.
5 I'm moving rooms. The noise is awful.
6 Paris is wonderful.

))) 6.5

1

C = check-in assistant, P = passenger
C: Can I have your passport, please?
P: Here you are. Do you need my booking reference?
C: No, that's fine. How many bags do you have?
P: Just one.
C: Could you put it on the scales for me? Thanks.
P: Could I have an aisle seat?
C: Certainly.

2

O = tourist information officer, T = tourist
O: Yes, madam. How can I help?
T: I need to go to the Hilton Hotel.
O: You could take the subway, the bus or a taxi.
T: How much is a taxi?
O: Around $50. The underground is only $6.
T: How long does it take?
O: Around 25 minutes.
T: Great, thank you.

))) 6.6

1

A: Good morning. Could you tell me the times of the trains from Ipswich to Cambridge, please?
B: There are two every hour, at quarter past and quarter to the hour.

2

A: What did they just say?
B: I'm not sure; it wasn't very clear. I think our platform has changed.
A: Which train are you waiting for?
B: The 12.05 to Naples.
A: Me too. Let's ask someone.

3

A: Where do you want to go to?
B: Brussels, but the machine isn't working.
A: Let me see … The machine won't take €50 notes.
B: Ah. Do you have change?
A: No, sorry, you'll have to go to the ticket office.

))) 6.7

P = passenger, T = ticket officer
P: What time does the 14.15 arrive?
T: The 14.15 gets in at 15.15.
P: Could I get a ticket for that train, please?
T: Sure. Single or return?
P: Single, please.
P: Excuse me, can you tell me which platform the 12.05 to Naples departs from?
T: The 12.05 will now depart from platform 12.
P: Great. Thank you.
P: Could I have a single to Brussels, please?
T: How would you like to pay?
P: By card, please.
T: Would you like a receipt?

P: Yes, please. Which platform is it?
T: Platform 4, but there's a 45-minute delay.
P: OK. Thanks.

))) 6.8

R = Rosie, M = Marek
R: Hi, Marek. It's Rosie here. Do we have a time for our meeting?
M: For both Magda and myself, Tuesday afternoon is the best. When can you get a flight in?
R: That works well for me. I can get a flight that gets in at 10 in Warsaw.
M: Really? That's great. I can meet you at the airport and we can fly on together to Katowice.
R: Great. Look forward to it!

Unit 7

))) 7.1

stopped, lived, wanted

))) 7.2

1
awarded
graduated
started

2
developed
finished
liked
produced
worked

3
managed
studied
trained

))) 7.3

A = Anna, M = Marc
A: What did you do at the weekend?
M: I stayed in bed in the morning, then I drove to meet Theo.
A: Did you do anything nice?
M: We just went for lunch. It was cheap so I paid the bill. How about you? What did you do?
A: I took the Metro into town and went shopping.
M: Did you buy any nice clothes?
A: No, I tried some on, but I didn't like them.
M: Did you buy anything?
A: Yes, I bought some books.
M: Did you meet anyone?
A: No, it was quite boring!

))) 7.4

1
S = sales assistant, M = Martha
S: How can I help you?
M: Is there a restaurant or café near here?

2
S = sales assistant, L = Luca
S: You look lost, sir.
L: I think I'm OK.
S: What is it you're looking for?
L: I need to buy a new laptop.

3

S = sales assistant, **D** = Da Long
S: Do you need any help?
D: Yes … Which floor are bags on?

·))) **7.5**

S = sales assistant, **D** = Da Long
S: Do you need any help?
D: Yes … Which floor are bags on?
S: They're just over here. I'll show you. … Are you looking for a particular type of bag?
D: I need a new flight bag.
S: Any particular size or colour?
D: The bigger, the better.
S: This is the biggest most airlines allow.
D: Great. Can I have one of those, please?
S: Certainly. Is there anything else?
D: I need to get some pens as gifts. Do you have any pens?
S: Just over here.
D: They look great. How much are they?
S: They're $15 each. How many would you like?
D: I'll take four, please.
S: Is that everything?
D: Yes, that's all thanks. Do you take credit cards?
S: Yes, but not American Express.
D: Is there a café near here?
S: The store has one, sir.
D: Which floor's that on?
S: It's on the top floor.
D: Great, thank you.

·))) **7.6**

1
Ch = Christina, **Cu** = Customer
Ch: Could I ask you some questions?
Cu: Sure.
Ch: Do you buy your food online or in a store?
Cu: I did my last shop online.
Ch: Do you always buy online?
Cu: Most of the time. I bought a few small things in the local shop.
Ch: Why do you prefer to shop online?
Cu: I like to get the food delivered – it saves me time. I drove to a store last month and wasted an hour of my time.
Ch: OK, great. Thank you for your time.

2
P = Paul, **C** = customer
P: So when did you last go shopping for food?
C: I bought some food this morning.
P: Did you shop online or in a store?
C: I went to a store.
P: Did you buy any food online in the last year?
C: No, I didn't.
P: Can I ask why?
C: I only shop when I need something. I don't buy lots of things at once.
P: Great. Thank you for your time.

3
Ch = Christina, **Cu** = Customer
Ch: Hi. Could I ask you both a few questions about shopping?
Cu 1 & 2: Sure.
Ch: Do you prefer to buy food online or in a store?
Cu 1: I prefer to shop online. I bought everything I need for two weeks in 20 minutes yesterday during my lunch break at work.

Cu 2: I hate shopping online.
Ch: Really? Why?
Cu 2: I like to look at the food and to see and feel that it's fresh. I don't want someone buying my food for me.

Unit 8

·))) **8.1**

Dal was unlucky with his first business project, the holiday dance for students. It failed not because it was a bad idea, but because it snowed! People couldn't get to the party because of the snow, so he didn't make any money.

The computer dating dance was very successful the first time, with four or five hundred people attending. But Dal spent all the profit on advertising. It didn't work. It was 1967 and the world wasn't set up for computer dating. People didn't use credit cards and they couldn't go online so no one was ready for computer dating.

Dal also tried to make a movie, but again money was the problem. He needed $1,000,000, but wasn't able to get the money because he didn't have any experience.

Dal's biggest mistake out of fifteen business failures was the drive-in disco. It was such a good idea that Coca-Cola offered $100,000 sponsorship, but he didn't close the deal quickly. He didn't work out the details and didn't sign the contract in time.

The idea that made Dal rich was a company called Tweezerman. He simply brought an idea from one market to another. He didn't have to invest any money and he didn't have to borrow any money. He simply bought the product from a supplier and sold it to shops.

·))) **8.2**

Ingvar Kamprad started selling matches, but went on to become the founder of the furniture firm IKEA.
Roman Abramovich started selling plastic ducks, but made his fortune in oil with the firm Sibneft.
Amancio Ortega first started working as a shop assistant. Today he owns the fashion retailer Zara.
Warren Buffet began selling chewing gum door-to-door, but made his wealth with the investment firm Berkshire Hathaway.
Sara Blakely is the youngest self-made female billionaire on the Forbes rich list. She started charging people to come into a haunted house, but today owns the successful underwear firm Spanx.

·))) **8.3**

T = Temi, **K** = Karl
T: I've been reading this book on success in business recently.
K: What is it like? Any good?
T: It's really interesting. The writer interviewed lots of people about the characteristics of successful people and then produced a list of the most important qualities. What do you think was top?
K: Hard-working?
T: No, that was important, but not number one. Try again.
K: Luck must be one of them. There are a lot of people with good ideas that never make any money.
T: No, luck wasn't considered important at all. It was actually one of the things they said wasn't important.
K: Really? Well, I guess no one is going to say 'I'm rich because I'm lucky'. What's number one then?
T: Honesty.
K: Honesty – are you joking?

T: No, it was considered the number one quality.

K: But there are so many successful and dishonest people. I don't believe that one. Anything else interesting?

T: Yes, apparently education isn't important.

K: Really? I'd like to see how many Sorbonne, Harvard and Oxford graduates are unemployed! Sounds like a ridiculous book if you ask me!

))) 8.4

C = chair, S = Simon, P = Peter

C: OK, so shall we get started? Simon, Sally isn't here, so could you take the minutes?

S: Sure, no problem.

C: OK, the purpose of this meeting is to look at finalising our marketing trips for the last quarter of the year. We only have $30,000 left in the budget and need to decide which countries we should visit.

P: Are marketing trips the best way to spend the money? Couldn't we look at other methods as well? Such as advertising in magazines and sending marketing materials to clients …

))) 8.5

C = chair, L = Luis, S = Simon, P = Peter

C: OK, so it seems like there are a lot of options. Shall we try to decide on some actual destinations?

S: How about agreeing on two main strategies first? It'll focus our research. I think the main options are; four or five short trips to places that are quite nearby – Europe, North Africa. Or two longer trips to destinations further away, perhaps China and the Middle East.

L: Definitely, without doubt. Our budget is limited. I'll look into the China trip if you want and find actual costs. I'm not sure $12,000 for a two-week trip is realistic.

P: I agree, because in a country so big you can have a lot of flights.

L: I see what you mean, but most of the important business centres are on the coast. Planning it well, you shouldn't have too far to go.

P: I don't know about that, even north to south is a long way, but could you cost it anyway?

C: Could you do that by the end of the day, Luis?

L: Sure, no problem.

C: Then Peter, could you email our European and North African sales reps? Try to find out who thinks the end of the year is a good time to go.

P: OK, will do.

))) 8.6

Z = Zafira, A = Alex

Z: Hi Alex, come in. How are you?

A: Fine, but busy as usual.

Z: Me too. Let's get down to business then. So Pierre wants us to put together a team of four.

A: Yes, why doesn't he just do what we always do?

Z: I think he wants us to spot some new stars.

A: Interesting. Well, in that case I'd like to recommend George. He's an assistant designer. He's very hard-working and creative.

Z: I think Benoît would be good. He's a Customer Service Manager. He only manages a small group, but he's very passionate and well educated. He's moved up the company very quickly.

A: Sounds like a star. Good to have some leadership skills in the group. I think we need someone with financial skills. Amy from my team is a Financial Planning assistant. She's appreciative of the skills of others and honest. She always tells you exactly what she thinks!

Z: Well, that'll help keep the more creative ones under control! We need someone who's going to help the group be efficient and organised. Emilie, our administration manager, is very disciplined and great at keeping everyone focused.

))) 8.7

B = Benoît, E = Emilie, A = Amy, G = George

B: OK, so what do you all think about the idea?

E: Um, sorry Benoît. Do we have an agenda to keep us focused?

B: Er no, Emilie. Sorry, I didn't write an agenda. I thought an open meeting would be more creative.

E: Oh, OK. Is George here today?

A: I saw him this morning.

B: OK, well let's get started. He can join later.

E: Sorry, could I just check what time we're going to finish?

B: I planned to spend the day here. Amy, can you?

A: Sorry, I can't do that – I have too much to do today.

E: Me too. That needed to be in an email or agenda sent in advance and not so late.

B: Sorry, I'll try to be more organised next time.

G: Sorry I'm late everyone. I didn't have the meeting in my calendar.

E: Sorry, I'm going to have to go in about ten minutes. I don't really have time for this last-minute meeting. We need to plan for the next meeting.

B: OK, George, could you bring some competitor box designs?

G: Sure, no problem.

B: Amy, could you bring a spreadsheet for financial planning?

A: OK, it does vary from project to project, but I'll try to write something.

B: Emilie, could you access everyone's calendars and plan a series of meetings?

E: Sure, no problem.

B: Great. OK, I'll write an agenda and send it through beforehand.

))) 8.8

B = Benoît, G = George, A = Amy, E = Emilie

B: So why did you get a box designed?

G: Well, the product needs a box.

B: Yes, but you were supposed to get samples from competitors. Not actually design a box yourself.

G: I didn't like any of the competitors' boxes. I think my design's much better.

B: Yes, but we need to make these decisions together.

G: Yes, but I'm the designer. Surely I should have the most input.

A: Probably, yes, but we should all have some input!

B: Where's Emilie?

A: I only got the agenda ten minutes before the meeting. So she probably doesn't know when or where it is yet.

B: Sorry, Amy I didn't remember until the last minute. How did you get on with the financial spreadsheet?

A: Sorry, I didn't finish it. I thought we would get minutes with action points. Also, I didn't know the deadline was now because I didn't know when the meeting was.

B: OK, OK. Sorry … Ah. Emilie! Perhaps we could ask you to take the minutes?

E: Um, OK.

B: Did you set up the future meetings?
E: No, I didn't do it.
B: Why not?
E: I didn't know the deadline was today.

Unit 9

◀))) 9.1

I = Isabel, **O** = Orlando

I: Hi, Orlando. How was your journey?
O: Good. Really great connections to get here.
I: Fantastic. Now, here's your access card. You should keep this with you at all times. When you arrive in the morning, you have to swipe your card here. The start time is quite flexible, but you have to be here between 10 and 4.
O: That's great, always nice to have some flexibility. I wasn't sure what to wear today. Do you have any rules?
I: We do. You can't just wear anything you want. You don't have to wear a suit, but you should wear a shirt and tie. I'm afraid you can't wear earrings though. Also, you can't smoke in the building – you have to smoke outside I'm afraid.
O: That's OK, I don't smoke anyway. Do we have fixed break times?
I: No, you can take breaks when you want. Lunch is one hour. Now, have you hot-desked before?
O: No, I haven't.
I: I'm afraid here you have to hot-desk as we don't have enough space. I'll take you to your desk for today now.

◀))) 9.2

I = interviewer, **G** = Gabriel

I: So Gabriel, you work in a large supermarket in São Paulo. How many people do you manage?
G: I manage just under 280 people. We currently have 279 staff.
I: What days of the week do you have to work?
G: I have to work five days a week, from Tuesday to Saturday.
I: Can you choose the hours you work?
G: No, I have to start work at 6.00 a.m. The store opens at 7.00 a.m.
I: Do you have to work nights?
G: No, I don't. A lot happens at night, but sometimes when I get to work, there are still 80 boxes of stock that have to go on the shelves.
I: Can you open later?
G: No, we can't. We do a lot of business before everyone starts work.

◀))) 9.3

I can smoke in my office.
Can you park at work?
Yes, I can.
No, I can't.

◀))) 9.4

Eusebio

Hi. I'm Eusebio and I work every day from 7.30 to 3.30. I like it that the manager doesn't start work until 9 o'clock. Very few people start before 9 o'clock, so it's very quiet. Also Diogo always answers the phone because his English is the best! I don't like dealing with the post so we leave it for Monica to do later! I often just get to relax with a magazine.

Diogo

Hi. My name's Diogo and I work from 7.30 to 3.30 every day.

I really like my boss because he lets us do whatever we want. The company has quite a lot of rules, but Youssef is very flexible. I don't like it that I am the only one who can speak English on reception. It means I have to do a lot more work than the others.

Youssef

Hi. I'm Youssef and I'm the manager of the reception and some of the administration team. I work from 9.00 to 5.00 most days. I think I have too much to do managing the reception and the administration. I like working with the administration team, but not the reception team – they're always fighting. I leave them to do what they want – it's only the reception so it's not really that important.

Monica

Hi. I'm Monica and I work from 12.30 to 7.30. I don't like being the only woman in the team. The men try to leave all of the administration to me! But I do like all of the people in the company. Everyone's always very friendly, stopping to chat.

◀))) 9.5

1

C = customer, **E** = Eusebio

C: Hi, I'm here to see Mr Kant.
E: You go to office.
C: No, Mr Kant is going to meet me in reception. Can you phone him for me?
E: No, Mr Kant no phone me.
C: No, sorry, could you phone Mr Kant and ask him to come to reception?
E: Mr Kant not here.
C: He's not here.
E: No, he in desk.
C: Oh come on. This is ridiculous!

2

E = Eusebio, **M** = Monica

E: Monica, phone.
M: I'm busy with the post. You answer it.
M: Are you going to answer it?
E: No.

3

M = Monica, **C** = Customer

C: Excuse me, I was wondering if you could help me?
M: One minute, please.
C: Sorry, but this is quite important. You can talk about the weekend another time!
M: OK! One minute.
C: Unbelievable! Did you just ask where she got her hair cut?

4

D = Diogo, **C** = customer

D: Hi, sir. How can I help you?
C: About time!
D: Have you been waiting long?
C: Twenty minutes!
D: Sorry about that. I'm not sure where my colleague is.
C: Well, he was here when I arrived. He ignored me and went outside to have a cigarette!

◀))) 9.6

M = manager, **Y** = Youssef

M: Youssef, we had a lot of complaints about reception last month.
Y: Really?
M: Yes, over twenty.

Y: But what about?

M: The appearance of the two guys in the morning.

Y: They do look a bit casual.

M: A bit! They look like they're on the beach. The second issue is the post. Letters go missing, parcels are late.

Y: That's Monica's job.

M: What? No, it's the job of reception. I have to say it also seems like it's Diogo's job to speak English.

Y: Well, he is the best at it.

M: True, but we do have language classes.

Y: They don't have time for them.

M: The lessons are only one hour once a week. You must be able to work out a system with the admin team as well. The last thing is answering the phone.

Y: Everyone's so busy, we need more staff.

M: So what's the excuse for the fight between Eusebio and Monica?

Y: Fight? What fight?

M: How can you not know? It's the only thing people talked about yesterday! I want a plan of action to me tomorrow to show how you're going to solve this!

Unit 10

))) 10.1

L = Lia, **J** = José

1

L: Hi José, have you got a minute?

J: Sure, come in.

L: I'm having some problems in my office. My colleague Salvo speaks so loudly on the phone. I don't want to say something because I'm new and don't want to cause problems.

J: Do you want me to say something?

L: No, that might be worse.

J: You could ask him to speak more quietly. Or how about wearing headphones and listening to music?

L: That's a good idea. I'll do that. Thanks, José.

2

L: Hi, José. Do you know how to use the accounts system?

J: No, I've never used it. Why don't you go on a training course?

L: When's the next one?

J: Let me see … It's in two weeks.

L: Oh, I won't have time. I'll just practise at home.

3

L: Sorry, José ... me again.

J: Hi Lia, come in. What's up?

L: I'm really struggling with all these deadlines. I don't think I can meet them. Have you been on the time management course?

J: No I haven't, but I hear it's good.

L: I think I'll book myself a place. I need help!

))) 10.2

1

F = Franck, **A** = Anya, **G** = Greg

F: It's a lovely day, isn't it?

A: It's wonderful. What shall we do?

F: Why don't we go to the beach?

G: OK, would you like me to drive?

2

S = Sally, **P** = Penny

S: Just look at those clouds. I'm not going out in that.

P: Come on. Let's take a taxi.

S: OK, but you're paying.

3

V = Victor, **A** = Anka

V: We haven't got any food in the house.

A: Really? We could get a takeaway.

V: Let's eat out.

A: That's a good idea. I'll pay.

))) 10.3

R = Rosa, **K** = Keiko

R: Hi Keiko, it's Rosa here.

K: Hi Rosa, how are you?

R: I'm well, thank you. I was just phoning about the proposed meeting. I really think it would be a good idea to involve everyone in the department.

K: It's a nice idea, but we really haven't got time. A meeting with everyone could last all day.

R: True, but how about setting up sub-group meetings beforehand?

K: That would be great, but a bit time-consuming again.

R: How about starting an email discussion list then?

K: If I were you, I wouldn't do that. It'll just fill up everyone's email box. One thing I would suggest is setting up a discussion board. People can just go on it when they have time.

R: Yes, I agree. Good idea. I'll set one up and send around an email.

))) 10.4

M = Maxim, **A** = Abdulrahman

M: Hi, Abdulrahman, come in.

A: Thanks for seeing me about this. It's so hard at the moment.

M: No problem. Let's think about what we could do. Have you spoken to each of them individually?

A: I have. It helped for a bit, but not for long.

M: Why don't you organise a team meeting?

A: I'm worried some of them will start fighting.

M: Is it that bad?

A: I think so.

M: Perhaps you need to get someone to come in.

A: Like a training session?

M: Yes, maybe someone to motivate them?

A: That might work. I'll look into it.

M: Or maybe an awayday. Nothing too expensive, but it might be good to look at some options.

A: OK, great. I'll look at that as well.

M: I'll send you a budget and some other things to consider.

Richmond

58 St Aldates
Oxford
OX1 1ST
United Kingdom

© 2013, Santillana Educación, S.L. / Richmond

ISBN: 978-84-668-1357-0

First edition: 2013

Printed in Spain
D.L.: M-5209-2013

Publisher: Ruth Goodman
Editor(s): Anna Gunn, Hannah Champney
Digital Publisher: Luke Baxter
Design Manager: Lorna Heaslip
Cover Illustration & Design: This Ain't Rock'n'Roll
Design & Layout: Oliver Hutton/www.zoomdesigns.co.uk
Picture Editors: Helen Reilly/www.arnosdesign.co.uk,
Magdalena Mayo
Art Coordinator: Dave Kuzmicki

Publisher acknowledgements:
The Publisher would like to thank all those who have
given their kind permission to reproduce material for
this book:

Texts:
p20 extract from 'How I work', an article from Fortune
Magazine, March 16 2006 ©2006 Time Inc. Used under
license. Fortune and Time Inc. are not affiliated with, and
do not endorse products or services of, Licensee.

Illustrations:
Acute Graphics, Alex Green, Mister Paul, Myles Talbot
and Richard Allen.

Photographs:
China Foto Press; Deposit Photos; Desktopwallpaperhd.
com; Oliver Hutton, Plainpicture; Press Association/ Bernd
Weissbrod, Rex Features Ltd/Everett Collection, Topfoto,
Tweezerman, Wikipedia Commons.

ALAMY/DC Photo, Inspirestock Inc., Corbis RF Best, View
Stock, Kanaan Alkhatib, Alex Segre, Steve Teague, Eric
Nathan, vanillaaechoes, Tim Hill, Greatstock Photographic
Library, Bon Appetit, Keith Morris, brimo, Jajub Michalak,
amana images inc., Rolf Adlercreutz, Alex Segre, Alvey&
Towers Picture Library, Gavin Hellier, British Retail, Peter
Alvey, Rebecca Erol, Photoedit, TAR-TASS, Photo Alto,
Design Pics Inc., Duane Branch, Jorge Royan: **ARCHIVO
SANTILLANA**; CORBIS/Yumi Kamasaki/Ocean,

Simon Jarrrat, Matthew Ashton, Jon Hicks, Sean Justice,
George Hammerstein, Simon Marcus, Zave Smith, Dan
Forer, Image Source, Helen King, Tim Hall, Sean Justice,
Laura Doss, TongRo, Photo Alto, Antoine Arraou, Kate
Kunz, Tom Grill, Brooke Fasani Auchincloss, Ken Sleet
Photography, Sean Justice, Michel Setboun, Randy
Faris, Paul Panayiotou, Min Chapman, Tetra Images,
Mike Kemp, Artiga Photos, the food passionates, Fior
Ruiz, Tina Hager, Lucas Tange, Tomas Rodriguez, Jordan,
Bernd Vogel, Imagemore co.ltd, Walter Lockwood, Simon,
Design Pics, Condé Nast, Hemis, Andrew Parsons, Ragnar,
radius images, Maximillian Stock, Ewing Galloway,
Matthieu Spohn, Ariel Skelley/Blend, Adam Haglund,
Love Images, Rubberball, Simon Marcus, Fabrice, Artiga
Photo, Hero; **GETTY IMAGES**/ Cultura, Dan Kitwood,
Terry Vine, OJO Images, Image source, Stock Image, Jon
Feingersh, Walter Hodges, Dana Hoff, Carlos Ghosn, Aldo
Acquadro, OJO Images, Tetra Images, Cultura Henglein
& Steets, National Geographic, AWL images, radius
images, Jonathan Savoie, age footstock, Bloomberg,
Photodisc, Ryan McVay, Cavan Images, Eternity in an
Instant, Mark Edward Atkinson, Denis Doyle, Matt Cardy,
2010 Bloomberg, Andersen Ross, Blend Images, Britain
on View, Don Smetzer, Gina Martin, Flickr, Peter Dazeley,
Alistair Berg, David Hanover, Erick Isakson, Walker&
Walker, Joos Mind, Ian Walton, Bloomberg, CBS Photo
Archive, Daly & Newton, Runstusio, Visage, Ryouchin,
Image Source, Compassionate Eye Foundation, Liam
Bailey, Thomas Barwick, PictureIndia, @symbol/Ed
Honowitz, Caroline von Tuempling, Jacobs Stock, Tim Hall,
PhotoAlto, Tim Robberts, Brand X, Bruce Ayres, Taxi, Jetta
Productions, Jordan Siemens, Jupiter Images, Goldmund
Lukic; **ISTOCKPHOTO.COM**/ kabliczech, sjo,rhoon, 4x6,
bunhill, John Woodcock, jsnyderdesign; **THINKSTOCK.
COM**/istockphoto, altrendo Images, Stockbyte, Polka
Dot, Photodisc, Brand X, photos.com, liquid library,
Comstock, hemera, Digital Vision, Zoonar, Bananastock,
Christopher Robbins, George Doyle, Jupier Images, Jack
Hollingsworth, Michael Bann, Zoonar

*The Publisher would like to thank the following reviewers
for their invaluable feedback on @work. We extend our
thanks to the many other teachers and students around
the world whose input has helped us to develop the
materials.*

Reviewers:
Angela Lilley, The Open University, Oxford, United
Kingdom; Manuel Hidalgo Iglesias, QUILL Language
Learning, Mexico City, Mexico; Marion Grussendorf,
ACADIA GmbH, Cologne, Germany; Paulo Henrique Vaz
Lopes, Cultura Inglesa Belo Horizonte, Brazil; Radmila
Petrova Kaisheva & Anna Rumenova Boyadzhieva-
Moskova, University of National and World Economy,
Sofia, Bulgaria; Andrew Archer, Independent Publishers
International, Tokyo, Japan